I Am Going is an indispensable resource. I encourage Pastors to get this book in the hands of every one of their members. The Lord will use it to not only revolutionize their church but advance the gospel to the ends of the earth. Let's go!

Mike Buster, Executive Pastor, Prestonwood Baptist Church

Jesus told His followers to "go and make disciples of all nations," but this can seem like a daunting task, or something that doesn't apply to the average Christian. In this book, Dr. Ashford and Dr. Akin have done a fantastic job in laying out both why we go, and what that looks like. I highly recommend it as a resource to help us understand what it means to live on mission.

Matt Carter, Pastor of Preaching,
The Austin Stone Community Church

I Am Going is a little book about a big topic—our lives and what we can do with them. It's easy to read, and exciting! And I pray that for you, it may even be life-changing.

Mark Dever, Pastor, Capitol Hill, Baptist Church

I Am Going assumes that as a believer, you are called to be on mission for Jesus—that's not up for debate. With that settled, Danny and Bruce walk you through the steps of clarifying your call. They help you think through and pray through the details. For some it will be a calling that takes you across the globe. For others it might mean building a friendship with the person across the hall at the office. *I Am Going* will help you live with Great Commission intentionality no matter where God has placed you.

Kevin Ezell, President, North American Mission Board

From page one you will be challenged by Theology and Missiology. A great book to place in your people's hands and pray it ends up in their heart.

Johnny Hunt, Pastor, First Baptist Church Woodstock

If we are going *after* Jesus we must go *with* Jesus and *for* Jesus. This practical and powerful book by Danny Akin and Bruce Ashford will move you to say, "I am going too!"

James Merritt, Pastor, Cross Pointe Church

I Am Going is a clarion call for selfless commitment to the kingdom of Christ and the mission of his church. Danny Akin and Bruce Ashford are the right voices at the right time, and this book is an invaluable encouragement to the body of Christ.

> **Russell Moore**, President, Ethics & Religious Liberty
> Commission of the Southern Baptist Convention

When a seminary president and a provost write a cogent book addressed to the local church, it is especially appropriate to offer a word of thanksgiving. Akin and Ashford demonstrate their concern for the local church by explaining in lucid, easily comprehensible language what it means to be a part of a genuine New Testament church. The auditor of this book will not only become acquainted with two of the finest academes who lead Southern Baptists today but will also be introduced to a thoroughly New Testament doctrine of the church and its mission.

> **Paige Patterson**, President, Southwestern Baptist Theological
> Seminary, Fort Worth, Texas

Here are two men with Great Commission hearts, from a seminary with a Great Commission heart, writing a book with a Great Commission heart. Learn from their words how to be an Acts 1:8 missionary. Learn from their hearts how God can use you to change the world.

> **Thom Rainer**, President and CEO,
> LifeWay Christian Resources

The God who saves us is the God who sends us. That truth is one of many packed into this little book that offers a theologically rich and immensely practical vision of the church's mission in the world. May God use this book to stir up your heart to join Him on His mission!

> **Trevin Wax**, author of *Gospel-Centered Teaching,*
> *Counterfeit Gospels,* and *Holy Subversion*

DANIEL L. AKIN AND **BRUCE RILEY ASHFORD**

PUBLISHING GROUP

NASHVILLE, TENNESSEE

978-1-4336-4320-0

Published by B&H Publishing Group
Nashville, Tennessee

Dewey Decimal Classification: 269.2
Subject Heading: MISSIONS \ EVANGELISTIC WORK \
WITNESSING

1 2 3 4 5 6 7 8 • 20 19 18 17 16

Contents

Foreword

Two thousand years ago, a small group of ordinary men turned the world upside down in an extraordinary way. A movement that began with eleven men grew to over 3,000 people in a day. In the next 300 years, that movement would grow to over 30,000,000 people. Staggering numbers like this beg the question, "How in the world did that happen?" And the answer is simple.

They went.

This small group of men heard a clear call from Jesus. "Go," he said. "Go to all the people of the world and tell them the gospel—the great news of how God gives eternal life to all who confess Jesus as the Savior of our sins and the Lord of our lives."

So they went. And the world was changed.

Two thousand years later, the call remains the same. It is just as clear to you and me today as it was to them then. To every man, woman, and child who has put their faith in Jesus,

Jesus has said, "Go." He has not called any one of us to come, be baptized, and sit in one location. No, He has commanded every one of us to go, baptize, and make disciples of all nations.

This call to "go" starts right where we live. The God of the universe has put each of us in the house, apartment, or dorm where we live, in the job where we work, and with the people who surround us. He has put us there for a reason. He wants the people we interact with on a daily basis to know how much he loves them and to experience the life found in him. Indeed, he has called us to go to them.

But not to stop there.

The call to "go" extends to wherever God leads. We live in a world where approximately 3 billion people don't even have access to the good news of God's love for them. Surely with that many people on a road that leads to hell who haven't even heard how they can go to heaven, God is not just calling a few Christians to go to them. Indeed, He's calling multitudes of Christians to go to them.

Such "going" is what this book is all about. Danny Akin and Bruce Ashford have given you and me a biblical, practical, simple guide to going right where we live and wherever God leads. So as you hold this book in your hands, my encouragement for you from its beginning is straightforward: don't read it.

Instead, do it.

In the pages ahead, you will be inspired to consider all the ways you might go in your life and work, with your church and family, from your neighborhood to the nations. But don't stop with just considering all these things. Take the next step and actually do all these things.

In other words, "Go." And as you and I go, who knows what might happen in and through our lives and churches? Might you and I be a part of a movement of God in the twenty-first century like we read about in the first century?

O God, may it be so.

David Platt
President of the International Mission Board

1

I Am Going

If there were an annual award for "craziest year in the life of an American college grad," I (Bruce) probably would have received it for the year 1998.

On October 20, I stepped onto an airplane to go overseas for the first time in my life. I had never been out of the country. I was a country boy, having grown up in a small town in rural North Carolina. And now I was flying to Russia, where I would live for the next two years. *I was going.*

Upon landing in the city of Kazan, I encountered a number of challenges. During the winter, the temperature averaged 10 below zero and sometimes dipped as low as 30 or 40 below zero. On the colder days, I could take a steaming mug of coffee outside, throw the coffee up in the air, and it would freeze before hitting the ground.

Now, for the most part, I enjoyed the food in Kazan. But there were other foods that took a while for me to embrace. For example, one morning for breakfast, I was served fish jello. Not JELL-O-brand jello, mind you, but gelatin (a block of congealed fat) with a welter of shimmering fish flesh inside. Or, to take another example, one evening at a restaurant I was served a local delicacy, fermented mare's milk. You heard me correctly; I was served something like buttermilk, only it came from one of Silver's relatives.

Most of all, there were spiritual challenges. I made my living teaching English courses for several universities in Kazan. As I got to know my students and eventually met their friends and relatives, I soon found myself having conversations about Jesus and the gospel.

Kazan was a fascinating city. Unlike most cities in Russia, more than half of its citizens were Muslim. Of the citizens who were not Muslim, many were atheists. Practically speaking, that meant that most of the people I met and most of the friends I made were either Muslim or atheist. I loved every minute of it. The people I met and the friends I made were wonderfully warm people. I ate countless meals and drank innumerable cups of hot tea with my acquaintances and friends in Kazan.

Just before moving to Kazan, I had sensed God's leading in my life to move to another country to be a witness for him.

I knew I could get a job easily in any number of countries, and could allow that job to be "a place to stand" from which I could minister to the people I encountered. So I ended up moving to Kazan, serving the community by teaching English, and finding ways to minister to the people I met.

Here's the kicker—they were fascinated with the fact that I was a follower of Jesus. It was a rare occasion that I had to initiate a conversation about Jesus. More times than I could count, they would ask me why I had a Bible out on the coffee table in my house or, even more straightforwardly, they would ask whether I was a Christian and why I was a Christian. I spent every day serving the students of the city of Kazan by teaching them English, and I spent nearly every evening and weekend engaged in gospel conversations and teaching Bible studies.

Often, late in the evening, after my dinner guests had left or the Bible studies had ended, I would sit at the window of my fifth-floor apartment. Just outside of my window was a mosque. As the snow fell on the mosque, I would reflect on how amazing it was that I—a country boy from North Carolina—was living in Russia. Even more amazing, I was able to leverage my English-language skills to serve the citizens of Russia and to open doors to speak about Christ.

I could see how God had designed this opportunity; it was his intention all along to help me find my place in his mission to save the world.

What Is God's Mission?

What is God's mission in the world? If we, as Christians, are supposed to love God and obey him, it would certainly help if we knew what he was up to. Fortunately, God has given us the Bible, a book that tells us exactly what he is up to!

If we are going to understand God's mission, the first thing we have to understand is that the Bible is not primarily a storehouse of random facts about God or Israel or the world. Nor is it primarily a collection of rules. Instead, it is primarily a fascinating and powerful story about God. This story is told in four acts:

1. **Creation:** The first act is *Creation*. "In the beginning, God created the heavens and the earth" (Gen. 1:1). God created the world and everything in it, and he called it "very good" (1:31). God loved and enjoyed what he had created!

    At the pinnacle of his creation are a man and woman. They were different from the rest of his creation because he created them in his image and likeness (1:26–28). Unlike the animals, they could be entrusted with managing the world God created (1:28), making families (1:28), and working to enhance the garden (2:15). Also, unlike the animals, they were moral and spiritual beings who were instructed not to eat of the tree of the knowledge of good and evil.

A good way to summarize the uniqueness of human beings is to say that they are spiritual, moral, social, and cultural beings who were supposed to use the totality of their lives to please God. And at the time of creation, they did please God. In fact, everything in the garden was just the way it was supposed to be. Adam and Eve had a right relationship with God, with each other, and with the rest of the world.

2. **The Fall:** The second act is the *Fall*. Just after God created the world, the Bible's story takes a dark turn. Adam and Eve decided to rebel against their Creator (3:1–7). Instead of loving him supremely and obeying him completely, they disobeyed him and sought to take his place on the throne of the world and the throne of their lives. They believed the lie of Satan that they could become gods. In response to their sin, God cast them out from the garden of Eden.

Being cast out from the garden of Eden represented the fact that things were no longer the way they were supposed to be. Adam and Eve no longer had a right relationship with God, with each other, or with God's world. Each of us, just like Adam and Eve, has sinned against God. Each of us, like Adam and Eve, experiences broken relationships with God, with others, and with the world around us. Our lives are characterized not only by God's goodness but by sin and its consequences. Even as we experience the beauty and goodness of life in God's creation, we also experience the ugliness and badness of sin and its consequences.

3. **Redemption:** The third act is *Redemption*. Immediately after Adam and Eve sinned, God promised to send a Redeemer, a Savior, to save them from their sins (3:15). This promise represents our first "peek" at the gospel. Throughout the Bible, God continues to reveal more and more about who this Redeemer would be until, finally, in the Gospels, we learn that he is Jesus!

Jesus—fully God in all of who he is—came to earth and took on full humanity. He was fully man and fully God. He lived a perfect life, but was crucified at the hands of sinful humans. When he died on the cross, was buried, and rose again, he was making atonement for our sins and providing salvation for the world. On the cross, he took the guilt for our sins upon his shoulders so that he could suffer the condemnation that we should suffer. When he rose from the dead, he rose as a victor, having paid fully for our sins and secured the future salvation of the world.

You Need a Savior. Pause for a moment to consider the reason we need a Savior. We need a Savior because each of us, just like Adam and Eve, have sinned against God (Rom. 3:23). We are born with the sinful disposition to love ourselves and our own desires more than we love God (Ps. 51:5). This disposition traps us in an ever-widening web of sins (Rom. 1:24). Because we sin we are condemned (Rom. 6:23). But because of God's love he sent his Son to save us so that we do not have to experience that condemnation (John 3:16).

When we trust in Christ for our salvation, God forgives us of our sins and begins the process of making us more like his Son (Rom. 8:29). This process of making us more like his Son is something that should happen daily (2 Cor. 4:16) and that involves the totality of who we are (Rom. 12:1). God intends for our salvation to shape not only our personal devotions and "churchly" activities, but also our family life, our workplace activities, and the way we speak and what we do in our neighborhoods and communities.

4. **Restoration:** The fourth act is *Restoration*. God's work of redemption reaches its goal when Christ returns.

When he returns, he returns as a conquering King. As King, he will fulfill his role as the judge over all humanity. Those persons who are not saved in Christ will be judged on the basis of their deeds, and will be condemned. Those persons who are saved will enjoy his good pleasure and will live under his blessings forever.

When he returns, Christ will invite us to live with him on the renewed cosmos, the new heavens and earth (Rev. 21–22). This new heavens and earth is the world in which we now live, except purged of sin and its consequences. Our life in the new heavens and earth will be a thoroughly social and cultural existence. It is social, in that we will live together with believers from every tribe, tongue, people, and nation (Rev. 5; 7). It is cultural, in that our existence will be characterized by cultural things, such as art, architecture, and song (Rev. 21–22). In this way, we will enjoy God's presence and favor and will live in unity with each other for eternity.

In summary, we can say that God's mission is accomplished through his Son's life, death, and resurrection. His mission is to save us from our sins and to restore his good creation which had been marred by sin. But what does that have to do with us? In other words, how should God's mission affect the way we live? In order to answer those questions, we will first look briefly at the way God's mission affected Israel and the way it affected Jesus. Only after that will we be ready to understand how it affects us.

What Was Israel's Mission?

You might not realize it, but what you believe about where Israel fits into God's mission is really important to how you will (or won't) live on mission. Between the garden of Eden (where act 1 and act 2 of our story took place) and Golgotha (act 3, the climax of our story), the story focuses on Israel's attempt to redeem itself from all of the consequences sin brought to the world. When we read the Old Testament, we often find it difficult to understand the point of it in relation to our own lives right now. After all, it is full of things like kings and queens, deserts and oases, horses and donkeys, swords and chariots. It turns out that one of the best ways to make sense of the Old Testament is to take a look at what Israel's mission was.

The first place to look is Genesis 12:1–3. In this passage, God came down to a pagan named Abraham and promised Abraham that he would bless Abraham's descendants so that Abraham's descendants could pass those blessings on to all nations. Abraham's descendants—Israel—were commissioned by God to be a conduit of his blessings to all nations. Later, he promised Moses and Israel that he had chosen them to be a kingdom of priests and a holy nation who would display his glory (Exod. 19:5–6).

God's primary blessing to Israel was the promise that the Savior would come from within Israel. In fact, God continually reminded Israel of this promise. This Savior would be a blessing to the nations (Gen. 22:18), an eternal king (2 Sam. 7:12–16), and one who suffers on our behalf (Isa. 52:13—53:12).

God also blessed Israel by giving them a set of laws instructing them how to live if they were going to be a blessing to the nations. The law was comprehensive in nature. It started with ten basic laws—the Ten Commandments—but expanded to include hundreds of laws covering the entirety of Israel's existence. The law showed Israel how their love for God could shine through in the personal, social, cultural, and political aspects of their lives. Everything mattered to God! Every aspect of Israel's life offered the opportunity to show the world God's greatness and his goodness.

In fact, we could describe Israel's mission as having five directions. God intended for Israel:

1. to direct their worship *upward* to him, allowing him to direct their life as a nation;
2. to look *inward* at their life as a nation, making sure that they loved each other as a way of reflecting God's own love for them;
3. to look *backward* to the time when God created the world (a time when man and woman had a right relationship to God, to each other, and to the world), so

that they would live with the type of harmony God had intended from the beginning;

4. to look *forward* to the time when he would send a Savior-King, who would save them from their sins and institute a new world order in which God would be worshiped and sin would be abolished; and

5. focus *outward* on the nations, making their own personal and national lifestyle so attractive that the nations would want to worship their God.

Going back to God's mission, we see that Israel's mission was supposed to line up with God's mission. God's mission is to save a people for himself and to restore his creation which has been marred by sin. Similarly, God wanted Israel to live its life in such a manner that people would want to be saved by their God. And he wanted Israel to live its life in such a manner that it would give the watching world a glimpse of what God's coming kingdom would look like—a restored creation in which there would be no more sin or consequences of sin.

What Is Jesus' Mission?

Jesus' mission picks up where Israel's left off. God fulfilled his promise to Israel by sending his Son Jesus to be the Savior, just as he had promised. Every aspect of Jesus' life confirmed that he was the divine Savior. He was born of a virgin, which signaled that he was God born in a human body (Matt. 1:18–25; Luke 1:26–38). He taught God's Word perfectly and lived a sinless life. He announced that God's Kingdom was arriving on earth, and that entrance into God's Kingdom required us to repent and believe on him (Mark 1:14–15).

Jesus ministered both through words and deeds. He didn't choose between words and deeds, but wove them together in such a manner that his life was a seamless tapestry portraying the goodness of God and his salvation. Here are three specific ways Jesus lived and proclaimed the gospel of the kingdom on his mission:

1. **Miracles:** He performed miracles which revealed the nature of the salvation he offered, the type of kingdom he was announcing. In his miracles, he showed his power over nature, demons, sickness, and death. Through each of these types of miracles, he showed that he was God. Take, for example, his resurrection of Lazarus from the dead (John 11). He showed the watching world that he was God (e.g., only God can raise the dead) and he provided a preview of the nature of his Kingdom (one in which there will be no death).

   The same goes for other miracles. When he calmed a storm, he revealed that he is the God who created the seas and controls them, and he previewed his coming Kingdom in which there will be no more storms.

When he healed a leper, he revealed that he is the Great Physician, and previewed his coming Kingdom in which there will be no more sickness. When he cast out demons from a possessed man, he revealed that he has divine power over evil, and the salvation he provides will eventuate in a kingdom where there is no more evil.

2. **Hospitality and Teaching:** He welcomed the sick and the sinful, enjoying fellowship with them (Luke 14:1–24). He taught the truth about God and salvation, and explained the nature of his Kingdom. Throughout his life, he was sustained in this type of ministry by fellowship with the Father and by relying on the Spirit to accompany him in his ministry.

3. **Death and Resurrection:** He was crucified (his heel being bruised by the serpent) and on the third day he rose again (bruising the head of the serpent). Through his crucifixion and resurrection, he accomplished the mission of God: he inaugurated the kingdom of God by claiming victory over Satan, sin, and death, and he secured redemption for God's image bearers and restoration for his cosmos.

Jesus' mission was unique. The primary thrust of his ministry—the atonement he achieved through his crucifixion and resurrection—cannot be imitated by us. However, the way he carried himself during his time on earth can be imitated by us. Just as Israel's mission was holistic, so was Jesus'. He ministered both through words and actions. With his words, he announced that he was the Savior and that all people must trust him for their salvation. With his deeds, he gave a preview of what type of salvation he provided—a salvation which would one day culminate in a new heavens and earth, one in which there would be no more sin and no more consequences of sin.

What Is Our Mission?

After Jesus rose from the dead, he appeared to his disciples and said, to them:

> "All authority has been given to Me in heaven and on earth. Go, therefore, and make disciples of all nations, baptizing them in the name of the Father and of the Son and of the Holy Spirit, teaching them to observe everything I have commanded you. And remember, I am with you always, to the end of the age." (Matt. 28:18–20)

In this passage, which represents Jesus' parting words to his followers, he instructs them to make disciples of all nations. How is this relevant to us today? It is relevant in that it encapsulates our mission! God intends for his people to make disciples of every nation including our own.

How do we make disciples of the nations? We do so by baptizing them in the name of the Father, Son, and Spirit, and by teaching them all of Jesus' words. Our mission is to teach people the saving words of God and to baptize them into local communities of believers—churches!—that will equip them to bring the whole of their lives into line with God's intentions for them.

What gives us confidence that we can do this, especially when many people will oppose us because of our message about Jesus' salvation? Our confidence is that Jesus is with us always, accompanying us as we make disciples, and that he will be with us "even to the end of the age." That last promise is a big one. He'll be with us until he returns again to defeat his enemies and purge the heavens and earth of sin and its consequences. In other words, when the dust settles, he'll still be standing. And because we belong to him, we'll still be standing also.

The thing that is so "great" about the Great Commission is that it encompasses all of the other commandments and commissions. When we teach people "everything" Christ commands, we are teaching them everything the Bible teaches. Every word of Scripture is a word of Christ.

Words and Actions

Have you ever heard the phrase, "Actions speak louder than words"? What about the phrase, "You might be the only Bible your neighbor will ever read"? Or, "Talk is cheap"?

It's true, we can act a long time before we speak, but words are just as important as action. God created the world in the beginning with words. Practically speaking, we obey the Great Commission using *both* words and actions. Words are important because, as Paul asked in Romans 10:14, how could a person trust in Christ without ever having heard about him? Words are necessary! Our actions are important also because, as Paul said to the Corinthians, "Therefore, whether you eat or drink, or whatever you do, do everything for God's glory" (1 Cor. 10:31). Actions are important because they should be evidence of our own salvation and should be a preview of what life will be like one day in the new heavens and earth, when all of our actions will be in conformity with God's will.

Consider the analogy of a hub and wheel, such as those found on old-timey covered wagons. Both the hub and the wheel are important. The hub is the center of the wheel and it holds the whole wheel together. If the hub is removed, the wheel collapses. Conversely, if the wheel is removed, the hub gets little or no traction.

In this analogy, the hub of Christian mission is gospel words, while the wheel is gospel-motivated and gospel-centered actions. The hub is essential because without it, the wheel collapses. This was Paul's point when he posed the rhetorical question: how could a person believe in Christ without hearing about him? This is why our mission is to speak words about Christ as often as we can and in as attractive of a way as we can.

The wheel is also essential. If the wheel is removed, the covered wagon would get little or no traction. This was Paul's point when he said that we should glorify God in everything we do. Why would we want our words to be shaped by Christ, but not our actions? Would we ever say that we wanted to speak the gospel to our neighbor, but also at the same time steal the money in our neighbor's savings account and treat his family poorly? Of course not. When gospel words are not accompanied by gospel-shaped lives, our words will often have little or no traction.

We could describe our mission, like Israel's, as being five-directional. God wants us to:

1. direct our worship *upward* to him, allowing him to make us more like his Son Jesus;
2. look *inward* at our family lives and church lives, seeking to love one another in a way that reflects God's love for us and for the world;
3. point *backward* to God's creational design for the world, a design in which humanity had a right

relationship with him, with each other, and with the created world;

4. live in such a way that our lives point *forward* to the time when Jesus returns to renew and restore the world into a new heavens and earth, the type of lives that serve as a preview of that coming Kingdom; and

5. focus *outward* on the nations, seeking to attract them to Christ so that they will experience the salvation he offers.

Our mission is *upward, inward, backward, forward,* and *outward.*

Conclusion

During the winter of 1999, several groups of college students and young professionals met with me in my Kazan apartment on weekday evenings and on Saturday morning. Most of them had asked if I would put together an informal gathering of some sort where they could practice their English. I had responded that I'd be happy to do so, but I wanted to center our English conversation around an ancient book, the Bible.

Most of them were not Christians, but they happily agreed to the arrangement. We began the evening with a potluck dinner. Each person brought part of the meal. One would bring the soup. Another person would bring fresh-baked bread. Another would bring the dessert. I provided the tea and coffee.

Over dinner, we did a lot of talking and even more laughing. Over these bowls of soup and mugs of tea, and through our conversations and shared laughter, we built friendships. After dinner each evening, we took out our Bibles and studied a passage of Scripture together.

I had designed a twenty-lesson Bible study that was intended to show how the Bible tells one overarching story, the story of a God who entered into history to love and save his people. Each week, my students—most of them Muslim—were assigned passages from the Bible to read. And each week, when it was time for our study, I would pose a number of questions about their assigned reading. The questions were intended to help draw out the point of the passages and to help each person to practice reading the Bible.

Over the course of months, our friendships deepened over countless mugs of tea and coffee. At the same time, our understanding of God and his Word deepened over the course of twenty lessons. By the time our lessons had ended, a number of them had come to believe the gospel. They trusted in Christ and made their commitment to him known publicly.

What was especially amazing was how they came to know Christ. They came to know him through words *and* deeds. They came to know him by listening to the Bible being taught and by reading the words of God for themselves. Through gospel words, they learned that Jesus is the Savior, and came to trust in him as Savior.

Along the way, they experienced gospel-motivated and gospel-centered actions also. They got a taste of Christian love and community during the Bible studies as they watched me and other Christians interact with each other and with them. They were able to spend time with some of these Christians outside of the Bible-study setting and saw the difference that Christianity makes in one's family and workplace.

As for me, I realized in a profound way that God could use a relatively inexperienced Christian like me as a witness for him. He used my job as a college teacher to bring me into contact with hundreds of students. Because of my job and the contribution to Kazan that it represented, I was able to meet hundreds of other people in the community. Because of some of the uniquely Christian characteristics of my life, many people were curious about my faith and asked me to share with them why I was a follower of Jesus.

In short, those two years in Kazan gave me a taste of the way that God would align me with his own mission in the years ahead. Did it matter that I was only in my early twenties, had never been out of the country before, and had never shared the gospel with people whose worldview was so radically different than mine? No.

What mattered is that God's mission is to save a people for himself, and that he had chosen to use me in this manner to accomplish his purposes.

Everybody is going somewhere. If I hadn't gone to Kazan, maybe I would have gone to take a job in Cary, North Carolina. Who knows?

The difference between living on mission with God, or not, is whether we evaluate our decision of *where* we go, *how* we go, *with whom* we go, and *why* we go in light of God's mission—the one who went before us.

Call to Action: Are You Going?

Clarify the Call

Be honest—list below the top three reasons why you *wouldn't* go with God on mission in a place like Kazan:

1. _____

2. _____

3. _____

Be honest—list the top three reasons why you *would* go with God on mission in a place like Kazan:

1. _____

2. _____

3. _____

Now, compare the first list to the second: What is the most compelling reason, either way, to decide where you are going?

Sign the pledge:

I, _____ *, will go.*

2

I Am Going . . .
with My Church

One of the highlights of my (Danny) life was doing mission work in South Sudan, one of the poorest and most dangerous places in the world. The reason I enjoyed my time there so much is that the Christianity I encountered was so real. The churches in that decimated nation are authentic. On the one hand they have next to nothing. On the other hand they have everything because their faith in Jesus is very rich. Let me share one specific example that I could repeat again and again.

In 2009 I joined a church team from Prestonwood Baptist Church in Plano, Texas, that went to Kajo Keji, South Sudan. It is a small town south of the capital of Juba and just north of Uganda. We were there to lead a Bible conference, conduct pastoral training, and do church planting. More than one thousand people from Sudan, Uganda, and the Democratic Republic of the Congo came for an incredible week of worship, training, fellowship, and church planting. Some of those who attended walked for a week to get there and then walked another week as they returned home. Almost all of the attendees slept at night on a blanket under the moon and stars. Seldom had I seen such happiness and joy in the Lord among brothers and sisters in Christ, many of whom had suffered greatly because of the civil war fighting in Sudan. One man in particular exemplified what we saw. His name is Pastor Sam.

Sam was born in Uganda. As a small boy, Sam witnessed the brutal murder of his parents and siblings by tribal terrorists who raided his village. He only escaped because he was able to run into the bush and hide. In God's grace a Christian family took him in. Sam put his trust in Jesus and was saved. As a teenager, he sensed God's call to be a pastor. We had the honor of helping Sam plant his first church. They quickly became a vibrant congregation that meets under several mango trees where they continue to this day!

This body of believers, who love Jesus and walk by faith in the most intimate and radical trust I have ever seen, has no building, seats (except the dirt ground and a few bamboo poles that I can tell you from personal experience are extremely uncomfortable!), screens, musical instruments, or any of the other trappings we in America so often think are necessary to *be* the church and *do* church. They do not look much like the twenty-first- century church in the US, but they have a striking resemblance to the church of the first century.

We cannot fulfill the Great Commission apart from the church. This leads me to ask three important questions:

- *What is the church?*
- *What does a biblically faithful community of believers look like? What does it do?*
- *How is a church to be a dynamic gospel outpost as it runs on the dual tracks of the Great Commission (the gospel to every nation) and the Great Commandments (love God and every neighbor)?*

Let's get after these important questions.

The Church *Is* . . .

When it comes to defining what the church is, there is a lot of confusion. Multiple usages abound, and there is a lack of clarity at a most basic level—understanding the very essence and nature of the church. We need to do some solid biblical thinking.

The church was born on the Day of Pentecost (Acts 2), though we recognize from Ephesians 3:14–21 the church of the Lord Jesus Christ is made up of all believers of all ages.

A survey of the New Testament reveals four clear uses of the term *church*. It is helpful to quickly identify each:

1. **The Local Church:** Most often the word *ekklesia* designates a specific gathering of believers in some definite locality. This is its primary usage in the Bible.

2. **A House Church:** Many local churches met in houses, and so they were called "house churches" (Philem. 2).

3. **A Collection of Churches:** The churches of a region, for example Judea, Galilee, and Samaria (Acts 9:31). This use is very rare.

4. **The Universal Church:** In some instances the word serves to denote the whole body of Christ, all believers throughout the world, those who outwardly profess Christ and organize for purposes of worship, under the guidance of appointed officers. This is an emphasis found in the books of Ephesians and Colossians.

The Church Is *Not* . . .

Just as it's important to remember that "church" can mean several different things, it's also important to remember what church is not.

1. **Not a Building:** Nowhere in the New Testament does the word *ekklesia* mean a building. The *ekklesia* of the New Testament is never a structure composed of bricks and mortar.

A statement such as "I pass by the church every day on my way to school" would make no sense to early Christians. The church is the body of believers in Jesus wherever they gather for worship, witness, and work. In the early days, gatherings were small, and believers, as previously mentioned, often met in homes (Rom. 16:5; Col. 4:15; Philem. 2).

2. **Not a Denomination:** The church is not a national organization or a denomination. The church is not a denomination either. However, needs can be met by denominations. There is no reason why individual churches should remain isolated, without real, visible union with other churches.

Biblical images and metaphors, such as the people of God, the body of Christ, and temple of the Holy Spirit, are one of the means whereby we learn about the essence and nature of the church. Our colleague John Hammett believes "this is the primary means by which we are instructed." In addition to the three images, Mark Dever adds, "The church is the herald of the gospel (as in Acts). The church is the obedient servant (drawing from Isaiah). The church is the bride of Christ (as in Revelation 19 and 21). The church is a building (1 Pet. 2:5; Eph. 2:21). . . . The church is the community of people who live in the last days inaugurated by Christ's earthly ministry and the coming of the Spirit."[1]

How Should We Define Church?

Article VI of *The Baptist Faith and Message 2000*, our denomination's statement of faith, provides an excellent statement on "The Church." It sets reasonable parameters for like-minded brothers and sisters committed to the lordship of Christ and the authority of Scripture, but it does not pin down issues of methodology and practice that the Bible does not address. We believe this statement provides a foundation for a healthy methodological diversity grounded in biblical and theological unity. The statement is as follows:

VI. The Church

New Testament church of the Lord Jesus Christ is an autonomous local congregation of baptized believers, associated by covenant in the faith and fellowship of the gospel; observing the two ordinances of Christ, governed by His laws, exercising the gifts, rights, and privileges invested in them by His Word, and seeking to extend the gospel to the ends of the earth. Each congregation operates under the Lordship of Christ through democratic processes. In such a congregation each member is responsible and accountable to Christ as Lord. Its scriptural officers are pastors and deacons. While both men and women are gifted for service in the church, the office of pastor is limited to men as qualified by Scripture. The New Testament speaks also of the church as the body of Christ which includes all of the redeemed of all the ages, believers from every tribe, and tongue, and people, and nation.

From this definition, let's make some observations about important aspects of church life and practice.

How Can You Find a "Real" Church?

If you've ever moved to a new city, you have probably had to look for a new church. If you live in the United States, chances are you had many options, especially if you live in a part of the country with a strong evangelical presence, like the South or the Midwest. Regardless, when you visit a new church, how do you decide which church to attend? If you are like me, you want to find a church that reflects what God described in his Word as a healthy church.

Here are some good questions to ask: What are "the marks" of a New Testament church? What are the marks of a healthy church? These two questions are clearly interrelated. What are the essential and nonnegotiable evidences of a New Testament church?

Throughout church history, brilliant thinkers have tried to answer these questions, so that people like you and me might have churches around thousands of years into the future—so that God's mission might continue on earth.

Theologians have debated the "marks," or attributes, of a true church for centuries. For example, the Council of Constantinople in AD 381 stated that as Christians "we believe in one, holy, catholic and apostolic church." Four adjectives contained in this statement deserve a brief explanation since at least one term ("catholic") is subject to misunderstanding:

1. **One:** The church is *one* just as God is one. The church as the body of the one Lord Jesus Christ is to be known for its oneness or unity. Christians should be characterized by their unity (Acts 4:32). The unity of believers is to be evident in the church and as a witness to the world. Divisions and disputes bring shame and harm our testimony.

2. **Holy:** The church is to be holy because God is holy (Lev. 11:44–45; 19:2; 20:7; 1 Pet. 1:14–16). As the dwelling place of the Holy Spirit, the church is made up of saints set apart for God (1 Cor. 1:2). Our holiness is at the most basic level Christ's holiness. His holiness should be reflected in the church's holiness

(Rom. 6:14; Phil. 3:8–9). Paul teaches, that "Christ loved the church and gave Himself for her to make her holy, cleansing her with the washing of water by the word. He did this to present the church to Himself in splendor, without spot or wrinkle or anything like that, but holy and blameless" (Eph. 5:25–27).

In this present age, the church will never attain a perfect experiential holiness. John Calvin put it well: "The Lord is daily at work in smoothing out wrinkles and cleansing spots. From this it follows that the church's holiness is not yet complete. The church is holy, then, in the sense that it is daily advancing and is not yet perfect."[2]

3. **Catholic or Universal:** The church is catholic or universal because it spans across space and time. It constitutes all believers of all the ages and reflects the nature of the true church. While every true local church is part of this universal church and is a church in and of itself, no local church can be said to constitute the universal church. However, the church in both its local and universal manifestations is the body of Christ and is to reflect Christ and honor Christ.

4. **Apostolic:** The church is *apostolic* because it is founded on the Scriptures given through the apostles. The gospel and "the faith that was delivered to the saints once for all" (Jude 3) has been passed down from the

apostles who were called to be with Jesus. Paul told the church at Ephesus that they had been "built on the foundation of the apostles and prophets, with Christ Jesus Himself as the cornerstone" (Eph. 2:20).

John Calvin, the famous Reformer, is well known for his saying, "Wherever we see the Word of God purely preached and heard, and the sacraments administered according to Christ's institution, there, it is not to be doubted, a church of God exists." Anabaptists and Baptists went further than the Reformers, insisting upon "a believer's church." The conclusion they reached was inescapable: the church must be composed of genuine believer members only.

This biblical basis for a believers-only, or "regenerate church," is so clear that it is difficult to understand how we ever lost it. It is also hard to understand why we minimize it today within many of our own churches.[3]

Putting Marks and Membership Together: 7 Essentials

A New Testament church will be identified or marked by particular distinctives. A survey of the New Testament will reveal some nonnegotiables. We highlight seven:

1. Believers-Only Church Membership

The Bible teaches that the church should be a "regenerate church." Meaning that is only allows *believers* to be members. The membership of the local church is made up of those who confess Christ as Savior and Lord and whose life gives evidence of conversion. It is a community of confessing sinners who covenant together under the lordship of Jesus Christ. It will call sin what God calls sin and it will fight against what God calls sin. A New Testament church will make it clear that church membership is a privilege not a right. There are requirements and expectations that are clearly defined and articulated when it comes to church membership. It requires an understanding of the gospel, public confession of one's faith evidenced by a clear verbal testimony and baptism, and a pledge to walk in the newness of life in Christ.

2. Believers-Only Baptism

In the New Testament, public confession of Jesus Christ as Savior and Lord was by baptism. An "unbaptized believer" is an oxymoron in light of the New Testament. Closely connected to but distinct from regeneration/conversion, baptism is the means whereby one declares publicly his or her faith in Jesus Christ. New Testament baptism involved a particular member (a believer), mode (immersion) and meaning (public identification with Christ and the believing community). It is a prerequisite to coming to the Lord's Table where we proclaim his death until he comes again (1 Cor. 11:17–34).

3. Biblical Accountability (Church Discipline)

Church accountability, or discipline as it is also known, is clearly and repeatedly taught in the New Testament (Jesus addresses it in Matt. 18:15–20, and Paul does so in 1 Cor. 5:1–13; 2 Cor. 2:5–11; Gal. 6:1–4; and Titus 3:9–11). Historically, Christians have viewed church discipline as an essential mark of the church along with the Word rightly preached, the ordinances properly administered, and regenerate church membership.

4. Word-Based Ministry

For those who believe both in the inerrancy and sufficiency of Scripture, there must be "faithful exposition." In other words, preaching must be biblical in content and dynamic in delivery, preaching that is expositional and theological on the one hand and practical and applicable on the other. We must advocate an expositional *method* with a theological *mind-set* under an evangelical *mandate*.

5. Biblical Leadership

Today our churches are exploring again the biblical nature of church government and church offices in terms of function and number, particularly that of the elder. This is a healthy development. Scripture never specifies the number of elders (or "pastors"), though they are almost always in the plural. The focus is on their qualifications (1 Tim. 3:1–7). The Bible is clear that a properly constituted church will have elders and deacons, who are appointed by the congregation.

6. Missions, Evangelism, and Discipleship

A faithful church must be known for its missions and evangelism. In our years of ministry we have become absolutely convinced of this truth: No church will be missional and evangelistic by accident. It must be intentional. Evangelism and missions must be a priority, and it must start with the leadership. We should train our people to be on mission with God. We should challenge them to evangelize without bias or prejudice, loving and going after the exploding ethnic and minority groups across America. The authenticity and integrity of the gospel is at stake.

7. Vibrant Biblical Theology

Healthy theology is a mark of a healthy church. Theology allows us to glorify God with our mind and obey the commandments of Jesus (Matt. 22:37–38). Healthy churches will produce and foster a positive theological agenda, not merely one that is defensive and reactionary. We must teach biblical doctrine, love biblical doctrine, and proclaim biblical doctrine.

What Is the Mission of the Church?

So far in this book, we have asked important questions about God's mission, Israel's mission, Jesus' mission, and even your mission. But what is the church's mission?

Bruce and I are a part of a seminary (SEBTS) that sees itself as a servant to the churches. As a result of that commitment and conviction, we have a mission statement that closely mirrors what we think the mission of the church is. Adopting our mission statement to fit the church, this is what we believe:

"The mission for the church is to glorify the Lord Jesus Christ by equipping its members to serve the body of Christ and fulfill the Great Commission."

There is a lot that could be unpacked from this sentence. Let's break it down in some basic propositions:

- The church exists to glorify the Lord Jesus Christ (1 Cor. 10:31).
- The church exists to equip its members to serve the body of Christ as each member does their part (Eph. 4:11–16).
- The church exists to fulfill the Great Commission (Matt. 28:18–20).

The mission of the church stands on a three-legged stool. We glorify God, do discipleship within the body, and make disciples outside the body among all nations, including our own nations.

We also believe that there are two biblical rails upon which the church lives out its mission as we move forward in extending the kingdom of God among all people for his glory and their good.

One is the Great Commission. The other is called the Great Commandment.

The Great Commission
(Part 1—The Gospel to Every Nation)

The *Great Commission's* best-known statement is located in Matthew 28:18–20. We find Luke's version in Luke 24:46–48 and Acts 1:8, and Mark's version in Mark 16:15. There is a brief Johannine statement in John 20:21. In Matthew we are commanded by our Lord to make disciples of all the nations, every *ethne*, teaching them "to obey everything I have commanded." In the process he promises us his presence, "always, to the very end of the age."

Those who are committed to the Great Commission rightly focus on the "outer edges" of lostness where the gospel witness is faint or nonexistent. And, we understand that our divine assignment is not to make converts but to make disciples. A vital and essential component of disciple making is plainly stated in Matthew 28:20, "teaching them to observe everything I have commanded you." Now, if ever there was a daunting task, there it is. After all, teaching a person everything Jesus has commanded includes 66 books, 1,189 chapters, and 31,103 verses.

My brain is already exploding and my heart is already sinking. However, Jesus teaches us that everything the Bible instructs us to do can be boiled down into two basic commandments. Wow! What a relief!!

The Great Commandments (Part 2—Love God and Your Neighbor)

The *Great Commandments* are found in Matthew 22:37–39. The command to love God with your whole being comes from Deuteronomy 6:4–5 and is known as the Shema. It was recited several times a day by devout and faithful Hebrews. It is at the very heart of the Jewish faith. Preeminently above all things, we are to love our God. Jesus says the second great commandment is like the first. The command to love our neighbor is found in Leviticus 19:18. Jesus provides a really good illustration of neighbor love in Luke 10:25–37.

> Bottom line: our neighbor is anyone in need. Racial, national, social, cultural, and economic barriers disappear because my love for my God causes me to love those made in his image just as he loves them. No exceptions. No excuses.

Conclusion

Today on planet Earth King Jesus is the head of a body that the Bible calls the church. It is truly an incredible organism animated and empowered by his Spirit. It has a mind that can think his thoughts and have his perspective. It has eyes that can see the needs of neighbors. It has ears that can hear the cries of the nations. It has a mouth that can proclaim the good news of the gospel. It has legs that can walk to the hurting. It has arms that can embrace those in pain. It has hands that can serve those in need. It has feet that can be blistered and backs that can be whipped, all for the sake of a King who did all of this for us and so much more. This body called the church makes Jesus Christ real to this world.

So, our goal is not to build buildings, grow budgets, merely acquire knowledge, or be captivated by current political and social agendas. No, our goal is to grow up men and women, boys and girls to maturity in Christ so that they think like

Jesus and live like Jesus. Our passion is to fill the earth with Christ, his gospel, and his kingdom. These aims are what sets the agenda for this body called the church. Any other agenda will fall short. Any other agenda is not worth having.

Call to Action: With Whom Will You Go?

The local church is the training center for mission—for getting the gospel to the nations. Churches send. Church members go.

Prayerfully consider signing your name to the following pledge:

I, _____ , will pray for my church for the next five weeks. I will pray for my pastor, who is the leader God has given our church. I will pray that my church will become, or continue to be, a healthy church. I will pray for my church to become a missionary-sending church. I will pray for a missionary movement to start with me, whether I am sent around the world or across the street—but I will go with my church.

Signature: _____

3

I Am Going . . . *to My Neighborhood*

God planted a passion for the Great Commission in my (Danny's) heart at the age of nineteen. I repented of my sin and trusted in King Jesus when I was ten years old. Unfortunately, I did not grow much in my faith during my teenage years, and few of my friends knew that I was a Christian. I still look back on those years with much sadness and regret.

Our God, however, is a faithful and loving Father who, as Hebrews 12:6 teaches, "disciplines the one He loves" (cf. Prov. 3:12). My heavenly Father got up close and personal in his disciplinary work in my life in the summer of 1976, putting me flat on my back for a month and train wrecking my college baseball career. I am so glad he did.

As I was recovering from a serious injury, a wonderful group of teenagers and young adults reached out to me and began loving me unconditionally in Christ. An older man named Jack Fordham taught me how to share the gospel and to start doing the work of a "soulwinner." I started going out on what we called "Tuesday Night Visitation" where we would go door to door and tell others about Jesus. We did not care who was in the house. If they were human, we knew they needed Jesus just like us. I, in particular, went to visit my friends from high school. The word soon got out that Tuesday Night was "spiritual hit man night" when Danny would come knocking on your door, so a number of my friends began to find a way to be away from home on Tuesday nights. At that time I did not have enough sense to go on a different night! It was a time of great spiritual growth in my life.

Then I came to a radically new understanding of just who my neighbor is.

It was in the summer of 1977. Our church was not only active in local missions and evangelism; it was also active in mission work thousands of miles away. For several years our church had adopted an Indian Tribe in and around Sells, Arizona, known as the Tohono O'odham Nation. Alcoholism and poverty were rampant among this tribe. The gospel witness was very minimal. I will always remember my fascination of standing at a religious shrine with Mary and a totem pole standing side by side.

We spent a week with the Tohono O'odham doing Backyard Bible Clubs and nightly revival meetings. We also drove out to villages, some as far away as 100 miles. Since there were no speed limits in the desert, we could and did make the trip in less than an hour! To say that this part of our mission was a thrill is a huge understatement!! During the week we saw a number of persons, particularly children, profess faith in Christ.

It was also on this trip that God called me into full-time gospel ministry. I really had no paradigm for what happened at a Monday night revival service, but I have never doubted what God did that evening in my life. That mission trip was life changing for me in so many ways. I now had a new sense of calling and direction as to my future service to Christ. I also came home with a new set of eyes as to who is my neighbor. My neighbor may live across the street, but he may also live across the nation or in a different part of the world. If they needed to be loved and cared for in Jesus' name, no matter *who* they were or *where* they lived, they were my neighbor. Jesus made this clear on one particular occasion when he spoke the parable of the Good Samaritan. It will be worth investigating what this text teaches us about neighbor love and how we can love others well in Jesus' name.

Who Is My Neighbor?

In Luke 10:25–37 we find the parable of the Good Samaritan. Jesus tells the story in response to a lawyer who, with less than pure motives, asked him, "And who is my neighbor?" (v. 29). The lawyer was looking to put limits and restrictions on his love. As my friend Sam Storms puts it, "He had rules that governed whom he would love and how far his love for someone might go. So if he can get Jesus to set boundaries on who is and is not his neighbor, he can say to himself, 'Oh I've loved other Jews' or 'I've loved my family, so I must be in a good place with God.' In other words, if he could get Jesus to answer his question by saying, 'Your neighbor is your friend' or 'Your neighbor is your blood relative,' the lawyer can boastfully say to himself, 'I've loved them. That must mean I'm okay.' He could then walk away feeling vindicated and proud of himself."

Jesus would not let him off the hook with such an impotent and shallow perspective on neighbor love.

There are four major characters in our story. First, there was the man on a journey, almost certainly a Jew. He is robbed, beaten, and left for dead.

Sam Storms makes a really good observation once again: "It's important to note that he was 'stripped' and 'half dead' (v. 30). In the first century, travelers were able to identify one another in two ways: either by talking to a person and taking note of their accent, or by observing their clothing. In the case of this man, they couldn't do either one. He had been reduced to a mere human being, without ethnic indicators or markers to alert passersby to his identity."

We next meet a priest, a religious leader, a man who is supposed to know and serve God. He should be loving and compassionate to others. He moves to the other side of the road and keeps on walking. He acts as if the wounded man isn't even there.

Next, a Levite came along. Levites were also religious officials whose responsibility pertained primarily to the temple. He followed in the footsteps of the priest and just walked on by.

Then comes the central figure in our story: a Samaritan. This would have caught first-century Jewish readers by surprise. It would have caught them off guard. Samaritans had intermarried with Gentiles and were viewed by Jews as half-breeds and false worshipers who had built their own temple on Mount Gerizim, insisting it was the only true place to worship God.

Jews hated and cursed Samaritans and prayed that God would never save any of them (cf John 4:9 and 8:48). To speak plainly, to a Jew there was no such thing as a "good" Samaritan. That was an oxymoron. It was nonsense.

Unlike the priest and Levite, the first reaction of the hated Samaritan wasn't self-protection or an instinctive turn to the other side of the road, but compassion. In fact, Jesus goes out of his way to note not only that the Samaritan did what the

Jewish priest and Levite didn't do, but that he also made up for the actions of the robbers.

They robbed him. / The Samaritan pays for him.

They leave him dying. / The Samaritan leaves him well attended to and cared for.

They abandon him. / The Samaritan promised to return.

The parable then concludes in verses 36–37 with Jesus driving home his point.

It is instructive that he reverses the question of verse 29. Don't ask, "Who is my neighbor?" Instead, ask, "Whose neighbor am I?" The question, "Who is my neighbor?" is the wrong question to ask. Jesus is saying that we can never conceive of any human being as a non-neighbor, regardless of his race, country, social or economic status.

The parable then is not really about the identity of your neighbor. The parable is about your identity as a neighbor (!) and a follower of Jesus. It is not about who our neighbor is but who we are. The question is whether or not you are the sort of person who sees yourself to be the neighbor of anyone who is in need.

Christlike love does not permit us to choose whom we will or will not love. We are forbidden from putting people into categories in such a way that we are only responsible to love "our kind," people we like, people just like us.

The kindness of those who follow Jesus must never be restricted, as if we are called to help and love only those who share our faith. We are to be neighbors to any and all who need to be loved, who need a touch of grace and compassion. After all, isn't that what Jesus has done for us?

(I want to credit much of this study to Pastor Sam Storms from whom I drew extensively. Thank you, good friend, for sharing your insights!)

Isn't the Great Commission for Missionaries?

Recently I spoke at a scholarly gathering. I playfully call such gatherings "the revenge of the nerds." Before you pass judgment on me, at least come and check one out for yourself. Jokes aside, I dearly love these scholarly brothers and sisters and thank God for their valuable contributions to the church of the Lord Jesus Christ. They bless us in so many ways.

The title of my paper was "Building Great Commission Families." My point was obeying the Great Commission is for everyone and that obeying the Great Commission should begin, but not end, in the home. Here is, basically, what I said:

> I want to be both biblical and strategic. For mothers and fathers, grandmothers and grandfathers, obeying the Great Commission should begin in the home, though it should certainly not end here. If the question is why, I believe the answer is clear and simple. It is biblical. Jesus informs us in Matthew 22:37 that the

Greatest Commandment is "Love the Lord your God will all your heart and with all your soul and with all your mind."

Most children look up to, admire, and follow in their parents' footsteps. What you love they will love. What you value they will value. What you have a passion for they will have a passion for. After all, you are their heroes!

When teenagers were asked to name their #1 role model, parents topped the list. In January 2015, Stageoflife.com surveyed teenagers on the topic of "unsung heroes." Parents ranked #1. In 1998, *Newsweek* magazine reported the same thing. The fact is our children do care what we think, they do listen to what we say, and they pay a whole lot of attention to what we do! So, in the context of the Great Commission, what do they hear you saying? What do they see you doing?

You see, the assignment to fulfill the Great Commission is not just for spiritual "special forces." It is for everyone, beginning but not stopping in our homes and with our own families. We must strive to infect the Great Commission into the lifeblood of our children that they may have a passion for that which is the passion of King Jesus. The Great Commission is for all of us, and it is to be pursued all of the time anywhere and everywhere.

I Am a Neighbor

In his discussion of the two Great Commandments, Jesus adds Leviticus 19:18 as a complement to Deuteronomy 6:4–5. Growing out of my love for God, I love my neighbor, those who have been created by God in his image. Neighbor is not used here in a restrictive sense. All of humanity, even my enemies, are in view (see again Luke 10:25–29).

Now, some hear the phrase "you shall love your neighbor as yourself" and wrongly think it is narcissistic. However, the more I truly love myself the more I actually will deny myself and love others. To love my neighbor as myself means I will serve the needs of others with all the energy, passion, and zeal with which I serve and attempt to meet my own needs. However, only by loving my God supremely will I be able to love others, "all others," genuinely. And, as I love others genuinely I demonstrate that I love my God supremely. No wonder Jesus said, "There is no greater commandment than these."

Several years ago a Bible scholar named Don Carson preached at Southeastern Seminary at a college conference that really helped us see what it means to love others. He also taught all of us a good lesson in hermeneutics, or biblical interpretation. He encouraged us to examine the context in which Leviticus 19:18 is actually located. There you discover that loving your neighbor as yourself means a lot! Among other things, it means that you will

1. care for the poor (19:10),
2. not steal (19:11),
3. not lie (19:11),
4. be fair in business dealings (19:13),
5. care for the deaf (19:14),
6. care for the blind (19:14),
7. deal justly with all (19:15),
8. avoid slander (19:16),
9. not "jeopardize" the life of your neighbor (19:16),
10. not "harbor hatred against your brother" (19:17),
11. rebuke your neighbor when necessary for his and your good (19:17), and
12. not take revenge or bear a grudge against others (19:18).

Wow! God does not leave it to our imaginations as to what he means when he tells us to love our neighbors as ourselves. You and I are neighbors, and this is what it looks like to show neighbor love.

I Am a Missionary

Paul wrote the book of Romans to a church he did not found and had not yet visited. David Platt, president of the International Mission Board, calls it an extended missionary fundraising letter! In Romans 15 he tells the Romans straight out, "I hope to see you in passing as I go to Spain, and to be helped on my journey there by you" (v. 24 ESV). In other words he wanted them to be on mission with him as he was a good neighbor to those who, as far as he knew, had never heard the gospel.

In Romans 15:14–24, Paul puts forth six marks of a Great Commission people. He describes the essence of a Great Commission people, explores the breadth of God's mission, and then emphasizes the urgency of the Great Commission call among God's people.

Let's explore these six marks:

1. **Focus:** The first mark of a Great Commission people is *keeping focused on the most important things amid many good things* (vv. 14–16). Paul was confident that the church at Rome was doing a number of good things. He notes that they were (1) full of goodness, (2) filled with knowledge, and (3) able to instruct (or "admonish") one another (v. 14 NASB). These believers embodied what it meant to live good lives informed by good theology.

Since Paul knew "the good" is always the greatest enemy of "the best," he took an opportunity to graciously remind the Roman church of their calling to be "a minister of Christ Jesus to the Gentiles." The word "Gentiles" (v. 16) does not fully capture all that Paul is describing in this context. A better translation of the word ethne in this context, also used in Matthew 28:19, is "nations." Nations is not a reference to political or national boundaries, but to peoples or people groups—persons with a distinct language, culture, and identity.

Paul knew that most Christians and churches do a number of good things, and we should continue to do most of them. But, like Paul, our challenge is for us to keep focused on the most important thing, making disciples of all the nations, all the ethnes. We must be neighbors to the nations as they come to us and we go to them.

2. **Awareness:** The second mark of a Great Commission people is *an awareness that introducing the nations to Jesus is an act of worship to God* (Rom. 15:16, 19). Holding missions and theology together helps us understand missions as a service of worship to our God. Keeping missions and theology together will also help us understand that a proper motivation for doing missions is gratitude, not legalistic guilt. As a result, we believe missions and theology must always be linked together. In fact, the greatest missionary who ever lived was also the greatest theologian who ever lived; his name was Jesus. Furthermore, the greatest Christian theologian who ever lived was also the greatest missionary who ever lived—the apostle Paul. It could be argued that Paul was a great theologian because he was a missionary, since you cannot have one without the other. Thus, any theology that does not issue forth in a passion for God, nations, and neighbors is not Christian theology.

3. **Christ-Centeredness:** The third mark of a Great Commission people is being *Christ-centered and boasting only*

in him (vv. 15:17–19). In this mission manifesto, Paul says he can be proud of his toil for God but only because of Christ (v. 17). Paul speaks of what Christ has accomplished through him to bring the nations to obedience (v. 18). Paul knew that being Christ-centered would radically impact how we think, how we speak, and how we live.

4. **Gospel-Centeredness:** The fourth mark of a Great Commission people is *never losing sight of the centrality and nature of the gospel* (vv. 16, 19–20). The book of Romans is a gospel book, and its theme is captured in Romans 1:16–17. Paul knew the power of salvation was not in him or any person. The power of salvation is in the gospel made alive in the lives of sinners by the Spirit of God (vv. 16, 19).

Paul's insistence about the power of the gospel begs the question: "What is the gospel?" Mistakenly, the gospel is assumed to be similar to what Mark Twain said about the church: "The church is good people standing in front of good people telling them how to be good." This is tragically wrong, and unfortunately many in our churches define the gospel in a similar fashion. For years Billy Graham lamented because he believed that on any given Sunday, 50 percent of those attending church were lost because of a faulty understanding of the gospel. Several years ago I had the privilege of spending some time with him, during which I asked if he still believed this. Sadly, he said, "No, I think the number is much higher than that."

The question remains, "What is the gospel?" Some helpful contemporary summaries are:

- A *Twitter summary:* "The gospel is the good news that King Jesus died and paid the full penalty of sin, rose from the dead, and saves all who repent of sin and trust him."

- A *clear contrast:* "Every religion in the world can be located under one of two words: do or done. Christianity is a done religion; we are saved by what Christ has done for us, not by what we do to earn salvation."

- A *striking declaration:* "The gospel is the good news that God killed his Son so he would not have to kill you (see Isa. 53:10)."

- A *wonderful promise:* "The gospel is the good news that the person who has Jesus plus nothing actually has everything." And, "the person who has everything minus Jesus actually has nothing (see Mark 8:36)."

5. **Urgency:** The fifth mark of a Great Commission people is *being consumed with the gospel reaching those who have never heard the name of Jesus* (Rom. 15:20–24). There is no greater evidence of neighbor love than this. It is common for well-meaning believers to say that "the light that shines farthest shines brightest at home," "missions begins with our Jerusalem and then moves to the ends of the earth," or "people are just

as lost in Arkansas, Oklahoma, and Louisiana as they are in Algeria, Oman, and Laos." Although these statements are well intended, they reveal a fundamental misunderstanding of the breadth of God's mission both theologically and missiologically. Missiologically, the issue is not one of lostness but access to the gospel. Theologically, this belief misreads the strategy of the apostle Paul and the methodology laid out in Acts 1:8.

Paul says that he fulfilled his gospel ministry from Jerusalem to Illyricum (modern Albania) (Rom. 15:19) and goes on to say that it is his ambition to preach the gospel where the name of Jesus is unknown (fulfilling the prophecy of Isa. 52:15) (Rom. 15:21). Then Paul boldly declared his intent to head to Spain, simply passing through Rome on the way stating, "I no longer have any work to do in these provinces" (vv. 23–24).

Paul's statement raises the question, "Are you saying all the neighbors who need to hear the gospel in these areas have heard?" or "Are you saying all the churches that need to be planted to reach the neighbors in these areas have been planted?"

Paul would certainly respond, "No" to both questions. Paul makes the case that because a gospel witness is already present in these places and there are places with no gospel witness, he is consumed with getting the good news to the places where the name of Christ is not known. The breadth of God's mission demands Paul's passion to become our passion.

6. **Everyone, Reach One:** The sixth mark of a Great Commission people emphasizes the urgency of our service in that *each person does their part to see the mission completed* (15:24). Paul insists that every believer is called to leverage their resources and talents for God's purposes.

Paul's desire was to take the gospel to Spain because they had never heard the name of Jesus, but he needed resources to do so. He called upon the church in Rome to be his helpers. So I am a neighbor and I am a missionary. Why, we might ask, are we not making better progress in showing missional, neighbor love?

Conclusion

James Fraser (1886–1938) was a brilliant student at London University with a promising future as an engineer. He was also an accomplished pianist. Yet, he left that all behind and went to work as a missionary among the Lisu people where he would spend the rest of his life. What brought about this major directional change in his life that many, no doubt, saw as crazy and irrational? What happened was he was given a little booklet titled *Do Not Say*. God used it to broaden his horizons and alter his perspective. He began to understand that his neighbor isn't just those who live across the street who need the gospel. His neighbor is anyone anywhere, who needs the gospel. There were no believers among the Lisu. There were no missionaries among them to tell them about Jesus. Someone needed to go and show neighbor love to these people who had zero access to the gospel. James Fraser went, and today it is estimated that there are three hundred thousand Lisu Christians in Western China and thousands more in Myanmar and Thailand. The booklet that moved Fraser to action? Here is the key portion:

> A command has been given: "Go ye into all the world and preach the gospel to every creature." It has not been obeyed. More than half the people in the world have never yet heard the gospel. What are we to say to this? Surely it concerns us Christians very seriously. For we are the people who are responsible . . . if our Master returned today to find millions of people un-evangelized, and looked as of course He would look, to us for an explanation, I cannot imagine what explanation we should have to give . . . of one thing I am certain—that most of the excuses we are accustomed to make with such good conscience now, we should be wholly ashamed of then.

Acts 1:8 provides a helpful pattern and strategy for gospel advance and Great Commission obedience. It tells us to work where we are but to not stay there. We want to be intentional in reaching our city, our state, our country, and the nations all at the same time. None of these particular targets is to be neglected. How we go about the task of gospel advance will vary from Christian to Christian and church to church. The key to biblical obedience is that we are actively doing something in our Jerusalem, our Judea, our Samaria, and the ends of the earth.

Here are some ideas for consideration.

- Create community groups that are intentional in inviting your neighbors to come. Have an eye out for internationals who are often afraid, lonely, and long to build friendships in this new country.
- Adopt a school and serve the faculty and students with the love of Christ.
- Make sure sermons, devotions, and other types of teaching is gospel centered and driven by the inerrant and infallible text of Scripture with emphasis on how to apply the text to the lives of different kinds of people.
- Adopt an unreached people group and an underserved megacity in North America. Regularly inform the membership about them, pray for them, and when applicable, work toward short-term mission trips to serve them. Encourage families to consider moving to those cities to be part of the core group for that plant.
- Partner with like-minded ethnic churches or missions in evangelizing immigrants and other underserved ethnic minorities, including migrants and other short-term workers.
- Plan/attend at least one evangelism training course annually for your church; consider inviting members

of other churches to participate, especially smaller churches.

- Develop a comprehensive strategy with your church for sharing the gospel with every person in your community with no regard to racial, social, or economic status. This may include things such as home-to-home evangelism, neighborhood block parties, servant evangelism projects, one-on-one mentoring, after-school programs, university campus outreach, innovative outreach events, neighborhood Bible studies, evangelistic mercy ministries, etc.

Call to Action: Will You Go Across the Street? The World? Both?

Fill in the blank, in light of what you have learned.

List three neighbors whom you long to reach with the gospel:

1. _____

2. _____

3. _____

Clarify the Call

These three neighbors are:

Local ☐

International ☐

Sign the pledge:

 I, _____ , will go to my neighborhood.

I Am Going . . . *to the Nations*

Several years ago my (Danny's) wife Charlotte and I were in Southeast Asia. We spent a week with precious brothers and sisters in Christ who are faithfully serving King Jesus in very difficult and, for many, dangerous locations. These men and women, along with their families, are heroes of the faith for me.

My assignment for the week was to minister the Word to them. I did my best to be a faithful expositor and theologian, and to encourage them in their divine assignment. However, Charlotte and I were the ones who were encouraged. We heard story after story of how the gospel is going forth tearing down the strongholds of the Evil One and setting free those who had been captive to sin and the false idols of darkness. With a genuine humility that shown like a brilliant light, one after another after another shared what great things the Lord had done and was doing. Even in the midst of personal tragedies and sorrows, they praised our King for his grace, his mercy, and his faithfulness. More than once Charlotte and I prayed and cried with our spiritual family.

However, one experience was not a good one. I cannot recall a time that my heart was pierced as it was on this particular night. Charlotte and I had asked several couples to let us take them out for dinner. As we were headed to our restaurant, our driver turned down a street where I was totally unprepared for what I saw. Suddenly on both sides of the road, for at least a half of a mile, hundreds and hundreds of prostitutes lined the sidewalks. Some could not have been more than eleven or twelve years old. They were actually dressed in seductive uniforms that were similar to what you would see in a private junior high or middle school. The faces of these little girls and women I will never forget. Sadness, emptiness, and hopelessness were etched across their countenance. Smiles, if there was one, seemed forced, lacking any sense of genuineness. Later I was informed that most of these girls and women had been deceived and basically kidnapped. Sex-slave traders prey on ignorant and unsuspecting parents, especially in rural areas, promising a better life for their children in the "big cities." As I looked into these tragic faces, it hit me. Somewhere they have a mom and a dad. Do they have any idea what has happened to their precious daughters? I was overcome with a sense of sorrow and despair I have seldom experienced. God, you must do something. We, as your ambassadors, must do something!

Later my friend Don informed me that once he and two others marched down what I call "prostitution row" giving out more than fifteen thousand pieces of Christian materials. Tracts, Bibles, and *The Jesus Film* were distributed to these ladies of the night. He shared with me that the women would chase after them, not to pull them into a "massage parlor," but to receive the materials telling them about Jesus. He told me the smiles of the women stood in stark contrast to the angry glares of the men who were there to take advantage of these unique and special creations of our great God. He told me as they walked back up the street after giving out all their materials they were startled to see *The Jesus Film* being played as videos in massage parlors. Needless to say, Satan took a serious hit, at least on this particular night, on one of the many prostitution rows in our world!

I have since discovered that the International Mission Board has a specific ministry to reach out to and rescue these ladies from the sex-slave industry. I learned we have openings but few laborers. Sufficient funds to send those willing to go has, of course, also become an issue. Granted, the work is dangerous and filled with risk. But where did we ever get the idea that serving King Jesus is supposed to be safe?!

The lostness and darkness of a world without Christ came home in a new and unexpected way the night I was taken down prostitution row. The need for God's people to get radically serious about the gospel and the Great Commission never seemed more urgent. The nations are crying out for hope, and we have it. The nations are crying out for deliverance, and we have it. The nations are crying out for life, and we have it. The nations are crying out for salvation, and we have it.

Do you need a little motivation to pray and work for the fulfillment of the Great Commission? Take a short ride down prostitution row. I think you will find it will be even more than you need.

Who Are the Nations?

This is a question that seems to have a rather easy answer, even if the answer changes a bit from time to time. The nations obviously are the various nations and governments located across planet Earth. Currently, early in the twenty-first century, there are 196 official countries in our world today. So these are the nations. Right?

Well, not if you are using the word in the way that the Bible does. God's Book has something different in mind, something that will take your breath away when you discover how many nations there are and how many have little or no access to the gospel of Jesus Christ.

As we noted earlier, the Lord Jesus gave us what we popularly call "the Great Commission" in Matthew 28:18–20. These were his last words before ascending back to heaven and his Father. Last words are meant to be lasting words, words that leave an impression and make an impact. In these final words Jesus commanded his disciples (that includes you and me!) to go and make disciples of all nations. The word *nations* is the Greek word ethne. We get our English word "ethnic" from it. This word does not refer to countries or political entities. Rather, it refers to what missiologist call "people groups." These are people with their own distinctive culture, identity, and language. Most English translations of the Bible will use the word *Gentiles* when translating the Greek word ethne, but the phrase "people groups" is more helpful in a missionary context.

Now, we need to raise and answer some very important questions. We will utilize data from the International Mission Board (IMB) and the Joshua Project to help us answer these questions. Both of these sources can be easily accessed online.

First, how many people are alive today on planet year?
Answer: more than 7.25 billion.

Second, how many distinct people groups are in our world today?
Answer: almost 11,500.

Third, how many people groups are unreached? By unreached we mean they have limited access to the gospel.

Answer: more than 6,800.

Fourth, how many people on planet Earth have no access to the gospel (called the "unengaged") or limited access to the gospel (unreached)?

Answer: 3.78 billion

Those statistics are staggering. They are sobering. It is mind-boggling to think that in our day, with all of our numbers, resources, technologies, and wealth, there are still people throughout the world who have never heard the name of Jesus or received a clear presentation of the gospel. Today, right this moment as you read these words, there are places on our planet where you and I could go and be dropped by helicopter or parachute and we could walk days, weeks, even months, and we would never discover a church and we would never meet a Christian. These are the nations that Jesus had on his heart and in his mind when he died on a bloody cross. These are the people groups that the Son of Man came to give his life as a ransom (Mark 10:45). These are the nations that he commanded us to disciple before returning to heaven. These are the men, women, boys, and girls who will be born, live, die, and go to hell without ever hearing the good news of salvation through King Jesus if we do not obey his final marching orders. The exclusivity of the gospel, the reality that there is salvation only in Jesus, is plainly stated by Jesus in John 14:6. It is plainly stated by Peter in Acts 4:12. It is plainly stated by Paul in 1 Timothy 2:5. There is one Savior, not many saviors, and that one Savior is Jesus Christ the Lord. And, there is only one gospel, not many gospels, and it is the gospel of King Jesus. This is the message the nations desperately need. Therefore the wonderful Baptist statesman and theologian Carl F. H. Henry was absolutely right when he said, "The gospel is only good news if it gets there in time." I imagine it was this truth that compelled missionary John Falconer to declare, "I have but one candle of life to burn, and I would rather burn out in a land filled with darkness than in a land flooded with light." The nations are lands filled with darkness. They are lands needing the floodlight of the gospel.

Counting the Cost

Is there a cost in being a Great Commission Christian? The answer is yes, but it is the same cost that comes with following Jesus as his disciple. Let's let our Master explain.

In Mark 8:34–38 Jesus lays out the essence of "the normal Christian life," the basics of discipleship. There the Bible says,

Summoning the crowd along with His disciples, He said to them, "If anyone wants to be My follower, he must deny himself, take up his cross, and follow Me. For whoever wants to save his life will lose it, but whoever loses his life because of Me and the gospel will save it. For what does it benefit a man to gain the whole world yet lose his life? What can a man give in exchange for his life? For whoever is ashamed of Me and of My words in this adulterous and sinful generation, the Son of Man will also be ashamed of him when He comes in the glory of His Father with the holy angels."

Sadly, in our day, what Jesus describes as the normal Christian life looks like "the radical Christian life." The North Carolina evangelist Vance Havner said it well with his usual wit: "Most Christians have become so subnormal that if they got back to normal, people would think they are abnormal." I think we could use a dose of abnormal Christianity in our day! Now, being Jesus' disciple requires three essentials all found in Mark 8:34.

1. **Deny:** First, you must deny yourself. You must give up the right to self-determination. You must live as Christ directs. You must treasure and value Jesus more than yourself, your plans, your comforts, your goals, your

aspirations. You must put to death the *idol of I*! You must say no to you and yes to Jesus!

2. **Die:** Second, you must take up your cross. You must die! Luke 9:23 adds the word "daily" because following Jesus involves a daily death. I must die day after day after day. Be honest: deciding to die is not *natural*. However, it is *necessary* to be Christ's disciple. And it is not a quick death. It is a slow death, a painful death. It is the death of the cross.

3. **Follow:** Finally Jesus says, "Follow me!" Are we willing to believe Jesus? Are we willing to obey Jesus? Are we willing to trust Jesus no matter what? David Platt, President of the IMB, speaks of giving the Lord Jesus a blank check allowing him to fill in the details. Can you do that? Can I do that? It will be radical, not comfortable, because it involves a death to the self-centered life. I must die to me if I am going to live for him.

If you save or treasure your life, your soul, above all else, you will lose it. The one who plays it safe and considers his existence more important than Jesus will lose both Jesus and eternal life.

In contrast, the one who loses or gives his life for Jesus "and the gospel" will actually save it! Only Mark adds "the gospel." Jesus plainly says that following him involves risking it all—safety, security, satisfaction in this world and life. But, he promises us that it leads to a reward this world can never, ever offer.

You see, there is a life worth *giving* for the glory of God *and the gospel*! It is a dying to self that others might live! It is risking it all for the sake of Christ and others! It is not safe! However, it is best and it is worth it. And, it is the normal Christian life! J. I. Packer says, "There are, in fact, two motives that should spur us constantly to evangelize. The first is love to God and concern for His glory; the second is love to man and concern for his welfare." Gospel gratitude compels us to count the cost and give it all for Jesus and the gospel.

Your life is now set free to live the normal/radical Christian life when you see death as reward, when you can say with Paul, "For me, living is Christ and dying is gain" (Phil. 1:21). John Piper calls Philippians 1:21 the Christian's win/win scenario. If I live I get Christ. If I die I get more of Christ. Either way I win!

Jesus asks in Mark 8:36, "For what does it benefit a man to gain the whole world yet lose his life?" The answer is *nothing*. In verse 37 he asks, "What can a man give in exchange for his life?" Again the answer is *nothing*.

Dietrich Bonhoeffer (1906–1945) understood what the normal Christian life should look like. The way may be hard, but the path and the end are glorious.

The cross is laid on every Christian. The first Christ-suffering which every man must experience is the call to abandon the attachments of this world. It is that dying of the old man which is the result of his encounter with Christ. As we embark upon discipleship we surrender ourselves to Christ in union with his death—we give over our lives to death. Thus it begins; the cross is not the terrible end to an otherwise god-fearing and happy life, but it meets us at the beginning of our communion with Christ. *When Christ calls a man, he bids him come and die. . . .* But it is the same death every time—death in Jesus Christ, the death of the old man at his call. Jesus' summons to the rich young man was calling him to die, because only the man who is dead to his own will can follow Christ. In fact every command of Jesus is a call to die, with all our affections and lusts. But we do not want to die, and therefore Jesus Christ and his call are necessarily our death as well as our life. The call to discipleship, the baptism in the name of Jesus Christ means both death and life. (Italics mine)[4]

All of us must learn how to die for Christ and the gospel so that we, and others, may truly live. Counting the cost is the normal Christian life.

I Am a Missionary

Charles Spurgeon said, "Every Christian is either a missionary or an imposter." Taken in isolation and thereby misunderstood, this statement could send us swooning on a spiritual guilt trip. We might as well just give up on this whole Great Commission thing. Why, if Spurgeon is correct, maybe I am not even a Christian! However, rightly understood, the statement still is challenging. But, it is also liberating! We need to get very transparent and practical at this point. Not every person will go to the nations, but every person has an important part in reaching the nations. And, when you do your part, you are doing the work of missions. You are a missionary. You are obeying the Great Commission. So, the questions we all need to ask are, first, "What is my part?" and second, "Am I doing my part?"

> Charles Spurgeon said, "Every Christian is either a missionary or an imposter."

I Am Going to the Nations

I am going to the nations first and foremost in prayer. Because my prayers reach an omnipresent God, there are no spatial or geographical limits on their reach! Through prayer, I can reach out and touch any and every people group on the planet. A. B. Simpson says, "Prayer is the mighty engine that is to move the missionary work." A. T. Pierson adds, "Every step in the progress of missions is directly traceable in prayer." I am going to the nations by going to my prayer closet.

I am going to the nations by giving. In 3 John 8 a man named Gaius is told that he is a "coworker with the truth" as he assisted missionaries sent out by the apostle John to reach the nations with the gospel. I love that. Today, Danny and Charlotte Akin are literally all around the world sharing the gospel with those who have never heard through our giving. William Carey asked British Baptists in 1792 "to hold the ropes" as he went to India. They held the ropes, he went down, and the gospel invaded enemy territory to reclaim that which rightly belongs only to King Jesus! We can all be "rope holders" by our giving. David Livingstone said, "Do not think me mad. It is not to make money that I believe a Christian should live. The noblest thing a man can do is, just humbly to receive, and then go amongst others and give."

Conclusion

Several years ago my wife Charlotte and I were in a Middle Eastern country to meet with some of the mission students at Southeastern Baptist Theological Seminary. We have an educational mission's partnership with the IMB called the "2+2" or "2+3" program. In short, students spend two or three years on our campus knocking out sixty hours of a Master of Divinity degree in International Church Planting.

On this particular trip we had a sharing session on Saturday evening. It was wonderful as we listened to all that God was doing in and through these students in very hard and, in many cases, very dangerous locations. In our group was a petite and quiet young woman whom I will just call Rebecca. She was as tiny as a mouse and just as silent. She never said a word, best I remember, until she was put on the spot by Dr. Bruce Ashford, who was teaching a class.

Bruce asked Rebecca to tell us about the ministry assignment God had given her, where she was, what she was doing, and what it was like. It was like pulling teeth to get her to talk! Yes, she was shy, but more than that, she was simply a humble follower of her Lord.

With much hesitation Rebecca shared that she was in North Africa in one of the most dangerous countries in the world. She had to be taken by helicopter to her ministry location because it was a long distance from the capital city and the roads were too dangerous. Rebecca lived in a refugee camp for orphaned teens who had lost their parents due to the civil war fighting in their country. There was no running water. There was no electricity. And she lived in a dung hut. Just to be clear, that is a hut made out of dung. We further learned that she was serving with the IMB with no male teammates. She had a couple of female companions who had just left, and she had been promised a couple of replacements in the near future. Oh, they would be women too. Praise God for our brave sisters in Christ willing to go to the hard and difficult places! And, shame on us men!! I think I should also let you know I later learned (Rebecca never complained about a thing) that Rebecca suffered from serious stomach and intestinal issues and was hoping to get some helpful treatments while she was with us.

To say I was impressed with this young lady would be a massive understatement. To say I came under incredible conviction would be the same. Here was a beautiful, young lady putting it all on the line for King Jesus. She had counted the cost and believed it was worth it. Like fellow missionary C. T. Studd (1860–1931), one of the Cambridge Seven, who served King Jesus in China, India, Sudan, and the Belgian Congo, where he died and was buried, my sister in Christ by the name of Rebecca believes with all her heart, "If Jesus Christ be God, and died for me, then no sacrifice can be too great for me to make for him."

God is not calling everyone to leave their home and cross the oceans and live among the underserved, unreached, and unengaged people groups of our world. Now, I believe he is calling more than are going, but there will always be a need for those back home who make it possible for those who have answered God's call to go to the nations to go. That was true in the first century and it is still true in the twenty-first century. Having said that, there is another fact I am absolutely certain of: GOD CALLS EVERY CHRISTAIN TO BE A GREAT COMMISSION CHRISTIAN!

Every devoted follower of King Jesus is called by God to obey and do their part in fulfilling Matthew 28:18–20. So, the question is, How do I do my part? What do I need to be doing to answer God's call to action?

Even if you do not go yourself, you can go to the nations. Remember, when we go with our church (chapter 2), we go together. As a sender, one who gives of your time, resources, prayer, and finances, you fulfill a vital role in going.

But if you do go, either in short-term trips or long-term commitment, you also have a role to play in sending. The missionary churches of the New Testament became sending churches as soon as they were planted!

Let me be very practical addressing both individual Christians and Christian families.

The Individual Christian

- Commit to the total and absolute lordship of Jesus Christ in every area of your life, understanding that Christ's lordship is inseparable from all aspects of the believer's life, including family responsibilities, business and professional, and recreational or leisure pursuits. Men especially need to respond to this challenge. It is time for men of God to step up and be the men that God saved them to be.

- Devote yourself to a radical pursuit of the Great Commission in the context of obeying the Great Commandments of loving God and loving others.
- Participate in a local church-sponsored evangelism training class and make this a regular component of the discipleship process in your life.
- Pray specifically for the nations. Utilize something like *Pray for the World* from *Operation World* to guide you.
- Participate in a North American or international mission trip sponsored by your church at least once every four years.
- Grow in giving as a faithful financial steward with at least 10 percent of your income going to your local church. However, see 10 percent as a place to begin in grace giving, but not the place to stop.
- Determine to exercise a greater level of stewardship through estate planning and planned giving, leaving a percentage of your estate to your local church and other Great Commission organizations and ministries.
- Give serious consideration to adoption and orphan care as a component of Great Commission living.
- Repent of any and all sin that has prevented you from being fully used by our Lord in fulfilling the Great Commission. This includes sins of idolatry, pride, selfish ambition, hatred, racism, bigotry, and other sins of the flesh that dishonor the name of Jesus.

Individual Families

- Fathers take the lead in modeling Great Commission Christianity and taking the primary responsibility for the spiritual welfare of your family.

- Parents educate your children and help them to cultivate a Christian-worldview way of thinking and living.

- Build gospel-saturated homes that see children as a gift from God and our initial mission field. Consider, in this context, the vital ministries of adoption and orphan care.

- Make prayer for and the evangelism and discipleship of your children a family priority.

- Develop strategies as a family for praying for, serving, and sharing the gospel with neighbors, coworkers, and others with whom family members come into regular contact.

- Adopt a different unreached people group each month and pray as a family (1) for missionaries working with the people group, (2) for the conversion, baptism, and discipling of countless individuals within the people group, and (3) for the establishment of biblical churches among the people group.

- Adopt a different North American church plant each month and pray as a family (1) for the church's leadership team, (2) for the conversion, baptism, and discipling of countless individuals in the church's region, and (3) for the birthing of future church plants from the church.

- Spend a family vacation participating in a local church- or association-sponsored mission trip.
- Consider setting up a mission's savings account for each of your children that would enable them to spend six months to a year in a North American or International Missions context soon after graduating from high school.

I am sure you can add some additional and even better ideas to this list. Whatever you come up with, determine that you will do something. You will not be disappointed. Life is an awesome adventure for Great Commission Christians.

Call to Action: Will You Go Where No One Has Heard?

Every Christian is called to go or to send. Every practical idea listed above is related to both going and sending. Both contribute to the big idea of the Great Commission: going to the nations.

Clarify the Call

I will become a *sender.* ❏

I will go to the nations *short term.* ❏

I will go to the nations *long term.* ❏

Sign the pledge:

I, _____ *, will go to the nations (as a Sender or a Goer).*

5

I Am Going . . . *to My Job*

One of my (Bruce's) first jobs was a summertime table-waiting gig at a fine dining restaurant in Greenville, North Carolina. Looking back, it is exceedingly humorous that I was hired at such a cultured establishment.

I had held down several jobs before. Starting when I was a teenager, I had worked as a part-time pen-cleaner at a pig farm, a janitor at a pharmaceutical business, and an industrial-strength weed-eater operator at a golf course. Nothing in that résumé suggests that the next logical step might be waiting tables at a tuxedo-uniformed fine dining restaurant that specialized in Mediterranean cuisine.

But how would this Christian faith, this love for Christ, translate into a table-waiting job at a restaurant? I wasn't sure.

I had never worked in a "secular" job that was people-intensive like this before.

It turns out that job was one of the best ministry jobs I've ever had, including jobs I've held since then, such as church planter, pastor, and seminary professor. Every morning before going to work waiting tables, I prayed for each of my coworkers and for the patrons who would eat at the restaurant. I also prayed for myself, that God would show me how to do my job in a way that served my coworkers and the diners well, and in a way that would allow me to speak with them about Christ.

I experienced many answered prayers that summer. I could tell a number of stories, but one story in particular stands out. Every evening, the wait staff and management would close out the restaurant by gathering around the cashier at the bar to cash out our tips for the evening.

The bartender was a guy named Russell. He was training as a MMA fighter and was a very outgoing and confident guy. I found myself intimidated by him, even though he was always friendly toward me.

One evening, after the wait staff had cashed out their tips, he asked me if I would stay behind for a few minutes. We sat down at the bar, and he started in immediately. He mentioned that everybody in the restaurant knew that I was a Christian, and that I was a different kind of Christian than he had expected.

"Why are you a Christian?" he asked. "What does it even mean to be a Christian, and why is it so important to you that it seems to be the most important thing in your life?" He mentioned that I came to work before everybody else, worked as hard as anybody else, and seemed to genuinely care about the wait staff and the patrons. He also knew I had shared the gospel with many of the wait staff, and that a couple of them had become Christians.

In that moment, I sensed that God was working in Russell's heart. Over the next couple of hours, on into the early hours of the morning, I shared with him the gospel and answered his questions. At approximately 2 a.m. that morning, he got on his knees, told God that he believed in Christ's work on the cross, and asked God to save him from his sins.

That moment is one of the best memories of my life. It is a great memory because I saw a man trust in Christ and be saved, right in front of my very eyes. It is also an indelible memory because God showed me his power and his ability to use me to minister to people, even though I was an unimpressive country boy in the midst of a crowd of cultured wait staff and well-heeled patrons. And it was a moment I will never forget because that was the first time it dawned on me that "non-ministry" jobs are actually "ministry" jobs!

Where Do You Spend Your Time?

Aren't we all grateful that "real ministry" is not limited to church jobs and that "real worship and obedience" is not limited to the Sunday morning worship services of our local church? Most of us spend the majority of our waking hours away from our church gatherings. If real ministry and worship was limited to our church gathering, that would mean that the majority of our life is wasted!

We are called to honor him as church members, family members, community members, and workers. The fact is that all Christians are called by God to honor him in at least four ways:

1. **Church Members:** We are, first of all, called to honor him as church members. Remember, we go "with our church." As we pointed out in the second chapter, God calls us to live in gospel community with our church. He disciples us in community, and not just alone as individual Christians. As we gather for worship on the weekend, and as we deepen our friendships with church friends throughout the week, God does his work in our hearts and lives.

2. **Home:** God also calls us to honor him by loving our families and taking care of our homes. Our calling to a family is the most basic of our callings and yet is a powerful way in which God does his work in us and through us. In our role as parents, we are the primary teachers and caretakers of our children, the primary avenues of God's love for them. Our love for our children is a

manifestation of God's love for his children. In our role as spouses, our love for our wife or husband is a concrete picture of the love between Christ and the church.

3. **Community:** Additionally, God calls us to be members of a broader community. God places each of us in countries, regions, cities, and neighborhoods. In each of those contexts, God calls us to play a role as his ambassadors. We enter into those contexts and convey God's love through our words and our actions.

4. **Work:** Finally, God calls us to be workers. God made humans to be workers. All of us work, and every workplace holds forth great potential for honoring God and ministering to other people. Often our workplaces provide our best opportunities to develop friendships with, and share the gospel with, people who are not Christians. Additionally, the actual work we do should be done as a ministry to God and to our community. Unless a job is illegal or immoral, it serves as a conduit of God's provision for the world, as a way God provides for his creatures.

What Are Some Examples of Workplace Ministry in the Bible?

The Bible provides numerous examples of people doing their work consciously as ambassadors of God. But before we give some examples, we should take a minute to reflect on the fact that God himself is a worker. The Bible tells us that he worked to create the world, and it depicts him as a happy worker, a satisfied artist, a joyful builder.

Because God created us in his image and likeness, it shouldn't surprise us that he created us to be workers also. When God created Adam and Eve, he instructed them to work in a number of ways: to till the soil, name the animals, and lovingly rule over his good creation. In fact, after God's initial work in creating the world, he now often relies upon us—his creatures—to do the work he wants to accomplish in the world.

That's right. The Bible describes our work as a partnership with God. Psalm 90:17 says, "Let the favor of the Lord our God be on us; establish for us the work of our hands—establish the work of our hands!" When we work, we should pray for God to work through our work.

Take, for example, the work of an *entrepreneur*, the woman described in Proverbs 31. She works hard, even into the night hours (31:18, 27). Her work benefits her husband (v. 12), her entire family (v. 13), people in the marketplace (v. 14), the poor (v. 20), and even the entire community (v. 23). Her husband and children recognize in her an example of godliness (v. 28). The Proverbs 31 woman is the biblical writer's idealized model, but real examples of that type of woman can be found in the life of Ruth (Ruth 3:11) and others.

Or consider the work of an *artist*, Bezalel, as described in Exodus 35. The story of Bezalel is found in the middle of a bigger story about the people of Israel. God has just delivered the people of Israel from slavery and given them the Ten Commandments. Now, in Exodus 35, God is providing a tabernacle for the people of Israel. The tabernacle would be a tangible reminder of God's presence, his holiness, and his mercy on the people of Israel.

During the tabernacle's construction, Moses said to the people of Israel:

> Look, the LORD has appointed by name Bezalel son of Uri, son of Hur, of the tribe of Judah. He has filled him with God's Spirit, with wisdom, understanding, and ability in every kind of craft to design artistic works of gold, silver, and bronze, to cut gemstones for mounting, and to carve wood for work in every kind of artistic craft. (Exod. 35:30–33)

Moses understood that Bezalel had been "appointed" by God to be an artist and had been endowed by God with the wisdom, understanding, and skill necessary to carry out that appointment. Bezalel used these endowments—wisdom, understanding, and skill—to do his art work for God's glory and for the benefit of the entire nation of Israel.

As Christians, we shouldn't be surprised that our workplaces can be shaped by our Christianity and that our jobs can be embraced as callings from God. As the Dutch theologian Abraham Kuyper once said, "There is not one square inch in the whole domain of our human existence over which Christ, who is Sovereign over all, does not cry, 'Mine!'"[5] He also said, "The Son [of God] is not to be excluded from anything. You cannot point to any natural realm or star or comet or even descend into the depth of the earth, but it is related to Christ, not in some unimportant tangential way, but directly."[6] Kuyper is right! There is not one square inch of our existence—jobs included—that Christ does not have authority over and that he will not leverage for his kingdom purposes.

> As the Dutch theologian Abraham Kuyper once said, "There is not one square inch in the whole domain of our human existence over which Christ, who is Sovereign over all, does not cry, 'Mine!'"

How Can My Workplace Be a Ministry?

The Bible tells us that God often does his work for the world through the work of his people. He provided for the poor through the work of the entrepreneurial woman of Proverbs 31 and for the nation of Israel though Bezalel the artist. But how, practically speaking, does he provide for the world through ordinary jobs that most people have today?

Consider, for example, the way God provides for hungry children. Usually, he does not do so by miraculously sending "manna from heaven." Usually, he does so through the work of a farmer on a tractor. But before the farmer ever climbs onto the tractor, he has relied upon the workers who built the tractor in a factory and the workers who packed the seeds he uses to plant the crops.

After the farmer finishes his work on the tractor, a truck driver takes the crops to a warehouse, where they are later shipped out to grocery stores. At the grocery store, the food is placed on shelves by workers and sold by cashiers. But before those grocery store workers could do anything, a contractor had to build the grocery store. And that contractor relied upon electricians, carpenters, and metal workers. And so forth and so on to infinity!

When God feeds hungry children, he does so through a vast and interconnected web of professions. The same thing goes for the way God often heals those who are sick, provides shelter for those who need a home, and provides enjoyment for those in need of recreation. Through our work, God conveys his love and provides for his world.

Additionally—and this is significant—when we recognize our role as conduits of God's love and provision, our work takes on new dimensions. We begin to do our work with excellence, because if we are the "hands of God" through our job, we want those hands to provide the best service or the best product possible. We look forward to serving our coworkers and customers, because we realize that our interaction with them is in one way or another an extension of our Christianity. We look for opportunities to speak the gospel (words of life!) to those around us, as we realize we might be the only person they know who would speak the gospel to them.

Our workplace, then, is a place of ministry. We should approach it in this manner, confident that, at least for the time being, God has placed us in this particular job for reasons only he knows entirely. Even if we have a hard time seeing how God is working through our work, we can be confident that he is.

Three Questions

Sometimes it is overwhelming to get a handle on how we can do our particular jobs in ways that honor Christ. It's a pretty tall task, because our jobs are complex and multifaceted, and because the Bible isn't a job-explanation manual! But there are some specific questions we can reflect on that will help us get a handle on how to honor God in our workplace.

1. What is God's design for this type of work?

At a very general level, God's design for every workplace is the same. He wants the people who work there to provide services or products that are in line with his intentions for the world, as expressed in his written Word. We should do our work in a way that is moral and that causes our community to flourish. We should be motivated by the gospel, and we should approach our work and our work relationships in a way that reflects our devotion to Christ.

2. How has this type of work been corrupted or misdirected by sin?

Every person in the world is a sinner, and every type of workplace has been affected by sin. Because people are sinners who direct their heart's worship to counterfeit gods (such as sex, money, or power) instead of God, it is natural that their work will be affected by the misdirection of their hearts. Every workplace is twisted in some manner by the harmful effects of sin.

3. How can I redirect my workplace toward God's design for it in Christ?

If our workplace has been misdirected, then we will want to figure out how we can redirect it so that it fits with God's intentions, so that our work honors Christ.

Take, for example, an entrepreneur who wishes to open a restaurant. To the first question, he might answer that God's design for a restaurateur is, at a minimum, to provide nourishment for its patrons, to treat its employees and customers as people who are created in the image of God, and to serve the broader community in an appropriate manner.

After reflecting on the second question, he might conclude that restaurants are misdirected in various ways. An owner might only care about the bottom line, and this love of money might lead them to be dishonest about the quality of their food and to pay their staff as little as possible. Or, if a restaurateur does not view his employees as people who are created in God's image, he might view them as objects. Instead of cultivating their talents, helping them to flourish as employees, and praying for their well-being, he might treat them a lot like automated robots who exist only to serve the owner as efficiently as possible.

After reflecting on the first two questions, the restaurant owner will find it easier to answer the third question. He will build a restaurant that serves nourishing food to the community and does so for a reasonable price. He will view his employees and customers as God's image bearers and treat them with the love and care they deserve. When he has the opportunity, he will speak the gospel to them, tell them the story of how he came to trust Christ, and in other ways point to Christ.

We think these three questions provide a helpful framework for any person who wants to figure out how to minister in and through their workplace. The questions are easy to remember, but we know that they are not as easy to answer and apply. We must ask God to empower us and give us wisdom, and we must work hard to figure out how to apply God's redemptive word to our workplaces.

How Will We Accomplish the Great Commission?

When Jesus commanded his followers to make disciples of every nation, he had all nations in mind, including our own nation—the United States. For those of us who live in America, he calls us to make disciples of our own nation.

But how will we do this effectively if we do not treat our workplaces as places of ministry? For many of us the majority of our waking hours are spent at our jobs. There is no better place to join God in his mission than our workplaces!

Conclusion

Back to the story about my job waiting tables. I had applied for that restaurant job because I needed to pay for college. During the summer, I was working as a part-time youth pastor at a nearby church but was not earning enough money to be able to return to college. So I walked into a very nice hotel in the city and happened to see a "wait staff needed" sign on the door of their restaurant.

I walked up to the woman at the hostess stand. It turns out that she was one of the owners. She interviewed me immediately and hired me for the job. She agreed to let me work double shifts most days in order for me to be able to pay my bills. Immediately, I was able to see this new job as a provision from God.

What I was not able to see immediately was the way in which my job as a table-waiter was just as much a ministry as my job as a youth pastor. In fact, the table-waiting job was uniquely special. I was able to serve the broader community of my city by serving their meals and treating them as human beings made in God's image. I was able to befriend and serve my coworkers for the same reason. And much to my surprise, I was able to share the gospel regularly, sometimes at the specific request of my coworkers.

Now, I am able to understand what the great theologian Martin Luther meant when he said:

> If you ask an insignificant maidservant why she scours a dish or milks the cow she can say: I know that the thing I do pleases God, for I have God's work and commandment. . . . God does not look at the insignificance of the acts but at the heart that serves Him in such little things.[7]

Now I can understand what the great preacher Richard Sibbes meant when he said:

> The whole life of a Christian . . . is a service to God. There is nothing that we do but it may be a "service to God." No. Not our particular recreations, if we use them as we should. . . . We should not thrust religion into a corner, into a narrow room, and limit it to some

days, and times, and actions, and places. . . . To "serve" God is to carry ourselves as the children of God wheresoever we are: so that our whole life is a service to God.[8]

Living consistently as Christians in our workplaces is not always satisfying, and it is almost never easy. That is because we live in a sinful world in which nothing—and certainly not our workplaces—is free from sin or its effects. But instead of taking the easy way out, we have the opportunity to take the Christian way forward.

We view our workplace as an opportunity to be a conduit of God's love and provision for the world. We do our work in such a way that it contributes to our community and treats people with the love and respect we owe them as persons created in the image of God. We take every opportunity to shape our work by Christian principles, to witness to Christ both with words and actions. In so doing, we can be confident that God is working through us and in us.

Call to Action: Will You View Your Job as a Ministry?

Clarify the Call

1. What is God's design for my work?

_____

_____

2. How has my work been corrupted or misdirected by sin?

_____

_____

3. How can I redirect my workplace toward God's design for it in Christ?

_____

_____

Sign the pledge:

I, _____ , *will go to my job.*

6

I Am Going . . . *with My Job*

After having returned from Russia in the summer of 2000, I (Bruce) began PhD studies. During the time of my PhD studies, I missed my friends in Russia, and even more than that, I missed the cross-cultural ministry I was able to do there. I did not, however, miss the fish jello.

During the time of my studies, I was hired to teach philosophy. As I was teaching and studying, I began praying that the Lord would open doors for me to leverage my job as a philosophy professor on the mission field.

Shortly after I began praying, I received a phone call from an American pastor whose church did mission work regularly in Romania. He asked if I would be willing to speak at a ministry conference in Romania and "maybe speak to the philosophy departments at a couple of the universities." I could hardly believe my ears! It seemed that God was already answering my prayers.

By the time I arrived in Romania, it had been arranged for me to speak at two universities, the University of Craiova and the University of Constantin Brancusi in Targu-Jiu. I'll admit: I was very excited. I was excited because I had been praying for this type of opportunity and surprised that the Lord had answered my prayers so quickly. In fact, I felt an adrenaline rush as I got up to speak.

But I was also intimidated. I was only in my mid-twenties at this time and had never presented a paper in philosophy, let alone at a foreign university. I was sitting in front of a distinguished faculty and some very smart students, most of whom were predisposed to disagree with most or all of what I was about to say.

In my lecture, I did not preach. I did not teach the Bible. I did my job, as a philosophy professor, to talk about the big questions that any society must answer satisfactorily if they would build a stable society. I knew that those questions could be answered most satisfactorily by a people who believed in God. For example, if there is no God, on what would a society base its morality? But instead of making an argument for the existence of God during the lecture, I simply raised questions, and hoped that during the Q&A time I could be more forthright.

As it happened, things went exactly as I had hoped. During the question-and-answer panels at both universities, students in the audience asked exactly the types of questions I wanted to answer. I was able to talk to them not only about building a stable society, but about my Christian belief and how that affected the way I did political philosophy.

At one of the universities, we were videotaped for a national television show. At the other university, my colleague and I were given honorary doctorates in law. For me, it was easy to see

> He had used my workplace vocation— philosophy professor—for his purposes.

God's hand at work in all of this. He had used my workplace vocation—philosophy professor—for his purposes.

That week was the first time I realized that God could reconcile two seemingly conflicting desires that he had given me. One was the desire to be a professor and a writer. The other was to be involved in serious cross-cultural ministry overseas. How could those two things go together?

It seemed far-fetched to me that those two things could work together hand-in-hand.

But with God, all things are possible. And one of the most fascinating developments in the Christian world right now is the large number of Christians who are asking God to let them take their jobs overseas. They want

> One of the most fascinating developments in the Christian world right now is the large number of Christians who are asking God to let them take their jobs overseas.

God to take their workplace vocations—teacher, businessperson, artist, or scientist—to other contexts so that they can minister in those contexts.

Some Biblical Examples

It is not like this is some new idea God has for the twenty-first century. He has always worked in and through his people's vocations. He has always placed his people in new contexts, and even foreign countries, in order to plant their lives there and do work that honored him. Three of my favorite examples are Joseph, Daniel, and Paul.

Joseph in Egypt (Management Consultant)

The Bible's account of Joseph's life is colorful. Joseph was born into a wealthy family and grew up as a spoiled and immature rich boy. He was his daddy's favorite son. His brothers despised him for this, so one day they decided to sell him to some traders who were carrying goods to market in Egypt.

Joseph ends up in Egypt, where the traders sell him to a high-level government official named Potiphar. In a split second, Joseph had gone from being a rich boy to being a domestic slave. You might think that things couldn't get worse for Joseph but they could, and they did.

Potiphar's wife decided that she wanted to seduce Joseph. She tried, but he ran away. Feeling scorned, she (falsely) accused Joseph of rape, and Joseph ended up in prison. By this point in the story, you might be thinking that Joseph's life story couldn't get any crazier, but it could, and it did.

When he was in prison, Joseph ends up receiving illumination from God so that he could interpret the dreams of Pharaoh's butler and baker. A while later, he is summoned to interpret the Pharaoh's dreams. Because of Joseph's dream interpretations, Pharaoh hired Joseph and placed him directly under himself on the organizational chart.

The Bible teaches us that, in the years after his youthful immaturity, Joseph had become a devoted man of God. And now God had placed him in the most culturally powerful workplace of all: Pharaoh's government! Joseph holds a most serious job in the most pagan of environments.

Joseph's job involved managing disaster relief for Egypt. If you'll remember, Joseph had interpreted one of Pharaoh's dreams, and Joseph had interpreted the dream to predict that Egypt would have seven years of prosperity and then seven years of famine. So Pharaoh hired Joseph to manage Egypt's food distribution during the years of famine. It turns out that Joseph was very good at his job. He served Pharaoh well by serving the citizens of Egypt well.

There is much more to Joseph's story, including a moving reunion story involving Joseph embracing the very siblings who sold him into slavery. But for now, we've told enough of the story to learn some lessons about going *with* our job to minister.

Let's summarize the lessons from Joseph's story by noting that God had grand intentions for Joseph, that Joseph's job was essential to those intentions, and that Joseph only found out those intentions by being obedient along the way. He viewed his job as a calling and did it as unto the Lord. He viewed his job as a way of loving God and loving his neighbor, resisted sexual advances by another man's wife, and persevered through difficult periods of his life, which included being fired and sent to prison.

Daniel in Iraq/Iran (Government Administrator)

Another Bible story that gives us insight into how God calls us to go with our jobs to minister in his name is the story of Daniel. Like many of the people of Israel in his day, Daniel had been taken captive by the conquering Babylonian king, Nebuchadnezzar.

The Babylonian rulers noted that Daniel was a sharp young man, so they sent him to the equivalent of an Ivy League university for three years. There he was educated in the history, literature, philosophy, and religion of the Babylonian Empire.

Upon graduation, Daniel rose through the ranks quickly and became an advisor for King Darius. In fact, he was one of three chief administrators for the entire empire. The Bible tells us that he did his work with excellence, so that he was "head and shoulders" above the other two administrators in terms of his job performance.

His character, skill, and work ethic began to grate on his colleagues. In fact, they were so irritated that they hatched a plan: they would convince the king to outlaw prayer! They knew that Daniel prayed regularly to his God, and that if the king outlawed prayer to God, Daniel would choose God over the king and Daniel would be punished.

Sure enough, after the king agreed to the plan (not knowing that Daniel's colleagues had devised the plan in order to hurt Daniel), Daniel did not stop praying. In fact, he continued praying, publicly at his window, three times a day. The king was forced to throw Daniel in a lions' den as part of the pre-negotiated punishment for breaking the prayer law, but God shut the mouths of the lions so that Daniel escaped unscathed.

There is much more to tell about Daniel, but we'll be satisfied to note several things about Daniel and his workplace calling. First, Daniel allowed his relationship with God to shape everything he did. He prayed to God at least three times a day and allowed that time of communion with God to give him the strength and wisdom to do his job faithfully and with excellence.

And, as a result of Daniel's faithfulness, the Bible tells us that King Darius sent a decree out to the whole empire. To the shock of everybody in the empire, the decree stated that Daniel's God was the only god who could save and whose kingdom would last forever. Imagine how unlikely this scenario was: the leader of the empire, who was also by virtue of that the spokesman for the empire's false religion, declared to the entire empire that Daniel's God is the one and only true God. And he did so based upon Daniel's witness in his "secular" job!

Paul in Rome (Mobile Home Contractor)

At this point, you might be thinking, *Okay, you've made your point by using some high-octane examples of people who rose to the highest levels in their workplaces. But do you have a more ordinary example?* The answer is, "Yes!"

There are many more "ordinary" examples, but I'll stick with one of my favorite examples, the apostle Paul. Paul was a missionary, a church planter, and a theologian. But he didn't make his living entirely by doing those things. He made his living primarily as a tentmaker.

In Acts 18:1–4, the physician Luke tells us that Paul designed and manufactured tents and brought them to market. From the history books, we know that tentmaking in Paul's day consisted of cutting cloth, sewing it together, and attaching ropes and loops. Usually this craft, like other crafts, was handed down from father to son. It is very likely that Paul's father taught him to make tents.

It is important for us to note that Paul did not stop making tents when he became an apostolic missionary. He continued to make tents and bring them to market. Most likely he used

Cicilian cloth (a cloth made of goat's hair) from his hometown of Cicilia, and very likely his tents were used by business professionals such as shepherds who needed a good mobile home.

When Paul made tents, it provided a salary for him so that he could do other things God had called him to do, such as being a church planter and a mentor to pastors. But it also made him a vital part of the communities to which he traveled and contributed to the welfare of those communities.

The Task Is Too Big! (But God Always Provides a Way)

As we have seen from the stories of Joseph, Daniel, and Paul, our God has always worked through people's workplaces to further his mission. He mobilizes workers strategically in order to accomplish his purposes. Our own twenty-first-century era is no exception.

In fact, we live at a time in which this type of workplace ministry is absolutely essential to what God is doing to advance his Kingdom. Two of the largest mission agencies in the world, the International Mission Board (IMB) and the North American Mission Board (NAMB) are increasingly relying on this type of workplace ministry even for their work in church planting and missions.

Take the IMB, for example. The IMB's stated goal is to make disciples and plant churches among every unreached people group in the world. There are unreached people groups in the world, and some of those people groups number in the tens of millions of persons. The IMB would need a baseline of at least twenty thousand missionaries just to have the most basic ministries in place among these people groups. At the moment, however, the IMB is only able to support financially approximately four thousand missionaries per year.

So if we were to base our appeal on financial limitations alone (and we don't), the IMB needs to recruit thousands of men and women to leverage their workplace callings for the sake of international missions. It needs businessmen to ask the international corporations for which they work if they may transfer to Asia, Africa, or the Middle East. It needs scholars and teachers to practice their craft in schools and universities all over the world. It needs athletes and coaches who are willing to compete and coach in other countries. And if God's people will be willing to fulfill their callings in other countries and contexts, the IMB stands a real chance of being able to make disciples and start churches among every unreached or unengaged people group in the world. Instead of four thousand missionaries, we could have forty thousand!

But our appeal is by no means limited to financial considerations. God's mission to save people from every tribe, tongue, people, and nation (Rev. 5:9–10) will necessarily involve Christians who are not "salaried religious professionals." He will need Christians who work in the arts and sciences, business and entrepreneurship, scholarship and education, and sports and competition. When a people group begins to encounter Christian witness in all of those spheres of culture, and when it begins to see the positive effects of Christians in all of those different arenas, they will be more likely to give the gospel a hearing.

This is the reason that NAMB's new church plants rely so heavily on workplace ministers. One of NAMB's "sending" churches (churches that send out its members to plant new churches) is the Summit Church in Raleigh-Durham, North Carolina. When they plant a church, their goal is to send twenty-five or more members of the Summit Church out to the new church plant. These Summit members move to the city where the new church will be planted. They find jobs, buy homes, put their children in schools, and offer themselves as the "ultimate volunteers" for their new church.

But how can a person leverage his or her job for the sake of church planting? The answer to that question is: "It can happen in many different ways!" But maybe it will be helpful to tell the story of two different families I know who took their workplace ministries to other contexts.

An Entrepreneur in Afghanistan

I am good friends with an entrepreneur whom I will call "Anders." While he was still in his twenties, he had already worked as a project manager for Fortune 500 companies helping with new business start-ups as well as turnarounds for large corporations. He had worked in that capacity for eight years and was very successful.

In 2003 and 2004, however, he began to sense that the Lord might want him to leverage his business abilities in a different context—Afghanistan. During those years the United States was at war with the Taliban in Afghanistan, and Anders knew that a war-torn country would need Christians who were willing to serve those who were in need.

After much prayer, he resigned his job and with his wife and two small children moved to Afghanistan. Between the years 2005 and 2011, he started a number of businesses in Afghanistan.

His first business start-up was a travel company. He wanted to find a market opportunity in which he could breathe life into a part of the economy that was underserved, while at the same time creating enough cash flow to set up several other businesses in the future. A travel company met both criteria.

The travel company was immediately successful. It bolstered the economy not only in the capital city, Kabul, but in the other cities and regions to which they helped people travel. It enabled them to make vast improvements on the safety of travelers. Significantly, it was also a business that put them in contact with lots of people. They were able to build friendships with people in urban, rural, and even remote areas. They were able to speak about Christ with the rich and the poor, the locals and the foreigners, the men and the women.

It also put them in contact with people of influence. They developed friendships, for example, with former militia leaders. One of them became a believer and eventually influenced many others in the valley to believe in Christ. Not only was Anders able to do ministry via the travel company, but local believers were able to work for the company and minister through it also.

The travel company generated enough capital that Anders was able to start other businesses. He started an English-teaching and computer-training institute in several of the places where their travel company worked. He started a media company that created TV and radio programs and broadcast them across the country. The media company's programming could not be openly evangelistic, but it could be shaped by Christian principles and it could provide openings and catalyze opportunities.

Because these businesses were well managed and founded on Christian principles, they served the community well. Because they served the community well, their gospel message was received more readily.

Just the other day, I came across an email that Anders sent years ago, where he reflected on what makes a Christian business a "Kingdom company." In the email, he listed four main characteristics of a Kingdom company. The email is worth reproducing in full, as it contains the raw and unfiltered thoughts of a courageous businessman who was writing an email to a friend late at night, expressing the need for more such businesses to be started. Here are the four principles, edited only slightly:

1. *Acknowledge that the company is God's, not our own.*
2. *Minister through our actions by showing how a Christian company is different than others. Make this a great place to work, because of what Christ has done for us. He blessed us so that we can bless others.*
   - Foster a management style that recognizes and honors the individual.
   - Treat our clients and suppliers like no one else.
   - Be dependable. Be trustworthy. Clients, employees, and suppliers should trust that we will do what we said we would do, and that we will do even more than that.
   - Be committed to a biblical ethic.
   - Invest in safety.
   - Develop the employee holistically.
   - Develop technical competence that allows people to be more productive and get promoted/be more efficient. This allows for a more successful career over time.

- Develop the employee as an individual through areas of interest—management training, soft skills, interpersonal communication.

- Develop outside educational opportunities, especially for field workers.

- Provide excellent health care.

- Reward people for good work. Give bonuses above what is expected, if unexpected profits come our way. Have them share in the rewards of their hard work.

- Create a fabulous work environment—this is where people are spending 1/3 of their lives. Quality of life matters! What little things can we provide for field staff that will make them feel better taken care of than any other company? What big things can we provide them? Create a vibrant work space for engineers and project managers. How can we motivate people to want to come and work here and stay here? Small and big things. Paint the walls, make it a beautiful open work space. Less institutional.

- Steward resources well—eliminate waste, but don't cut abuse or overload your work force. "For the Scripture says, 'Do not muzzle an ox while it is treading out the grain, and the worker is worthy of his wages'" (1 Tim. 5:18).

- Encourage people to take care of their health—fitness is important. Offer fitness benefits.
- Take care of their kids—this will mean more than anything else! How can we do this?
- Promote from within, open up career opportunities for current staff. Celebrate people who advance.

3. *Minister through God's Word. Expose people to the gospel, no matter whether they are customers, suppliers, or employees.*

4. *Minister through the provision of financial resources.* This is the icing on the cake. This is not merely a Business for Mission. It is a Kingdom business, where everything we do is to bring glory to God. When we are operating in a way that brings honor to God, then we can freely give away the excess. Employees will not feel that they are being abused if we have taken care of them in a God-honoring manner, and then we give away from the blessing and overflow of what God has sent our way.

Through multiple Kingdom businesses, Anders and his family partnered with several mission agencies in the area, including the IMB. They did things that no ordinary church planter or missionary could have done. They made a huge investment into the spiritual and physical well-being of the people of Afghanistan, and did so through their workplace calling.

A Chemist in Cambodia

Shortly after I stepped off the plane during a trip to Cambodia, I met an American couple whom I will call Marty and Wanda. Like Anders, above, Marty had been a successful professional for many years. Unlike Anders, however, he was a chemist.

For a number of years, he and Wanda had been asking the Lord's guidance in their lives, and wondering if there might be something different in store for them. Eventually, they sensed the Lord leading them to move to Cambodia to found and direct a major health initiative for an underserved people group.

In addition to serving the community through this health initiative, he and Wanda became a magnet for people interested in the gospel. Soon after arriving, they set up "Bible-telling" forums at their house. During these evenings they would tell the main stories of the Bible to their audience, which was composed of oral learners (people who do not read or who do their primary learning through oral rather than written means). Because those in the audience could not read the Bible for themselves, Marty and Wanda helped them to memorize the stories so that they could retell the stories to their families and friends.

But Mary and Wanda also connected with a number of other Christians in the area and were able to help facilitate those Christians' ministries. They helped support, for example, a Cambodian believer whose life goal was to win entire Cambodian families to Christ.

I asked for the opportunity to meet this Cambodian believer. When Marty introduced him to me, he began to tell me all about his ministry. He explained that he spent most of his time discipling fathers, who in turn would disciple their families. "After I do that," he said, "I just watch the gospel travel. These families will share the gospel with their extended families in other villages. Those families come to Christ and then lead others to believe in him also."

Marty and Wanda's ministry was fascinating to me. How often does a successful scientist pack his bags with his family and move to another country with the express purpose of leveraging his scientific abilities for the gospel? Marty and Wanda were able to found and direct a health initiative that served the public good. They were able to teach the Bible to unbelievers in the "Bible-telling" meetings at their house, and they were able to support Cambodian believers who were leading fruitful evangelistic ministries.

Conclusion

In all likelihood, the world outside of the United States would be interested in your field of work. I know what you're thinking: "I am not the CEO. I can't make my company send me to Saudi Arabia." And I would not suggest that is, necessarily, what you should do.

But I am suggesting that you consider, possibly, applying for a job overseas, in the same field. You might be amazed at how many international companies are interested in hiring American, English-speaking employees.

Or maybe your company has an office in another country. Could you work in the same job, in another context? What if your family was on mission, just like you are in the United States, an unreached country? You don't have to be a preacher to go with your job. You have to be who you are—engineer, marketer, lawyer, contractor, or farmer.

There is a man named Joey Lankford from Franklin, Tennessee, one of the most affluent communities in the South. Joey had a great, comfortable life, which he wrote about in a book called *Fulfilled*. But Joey was anything but fulfilled; he became increasingly discontent with a well-paying job, great family, great church—life as usual. It wasn't that Joey was unappreciative of the good life—he was actually very grateful—it's that he sensed something was missing.

So Joey did what any reasonable person would do—he walked away from comfort. Joey used his business acumen to begin a new business. His business was real—he was accountable to a budget, investors, and employees. This wasn't a vehicle for another, more spiritual plan. His job was the spiritual strategy! Joey hired men in South Africa to train to farm in his business, and deployed them to go start their own enterprise in their home towns. Vegetables, livestock—these were the tools God used not only to support Joey and his family financially, but to see men and women believe in Christ and call him Lord for the first time.

You can go with your job. Will you?

Call to Action: Will You Leverage Your Workplace Calling for the Sake of International Missions?

Clarify the Call

1. Does my job enable me to go?

2. Is it possible that the Lord might be leading me into a new career path? One that would enable me to go with my job?

Sign the pledge:

I, _____, *will go with my job, or send others who can.*

7

I Am Going . . . *Anywhere*

Sometimes God has to teach us lessons that he has already taught us many times before. This is especially true when it comes to our obedience in the area of gospel witness. Even though God has given to us the high responsibility and privilege of being the conduits though which the gospel is spoken and promoted, we tend to lose our focus and—sometimes, even—our motivation.

I (Bruce) regret that God often has to chasten me for losing my focus and even my motivation. One especially poignant memory of God's chastening is a trip I took to Europe a few years ago.

I confess that, when I travel, my natural inclination is not to talk with fellow passengers. This is partly because I am an introvert, but also because travel weeks are the busiest weeks, and I prefer to get work done while in flight. In my dream world, I would be able to board the plane, stow my bags, and spend the entirety of the flight answering e-mails, working on my lecture notes, or completing a writing project.

On this particular trip, the first leg of the flight was to Paris. Delta Airlines had just upgraded me to business class. I was seated in my very comfortable reclining seat. The flight attendant had brought me a glass of Diet Coke, and I was settled in to read a book by the philosopher Immanuel Kant in preparation for a course I was teaching. The book, *The Critique of Pure Reason*, is one of the most difficult to comprehend of any of the great books in Western history. It would take all of my powers of concentration to understand what Kant was saying so that I could distill his thought in my lectures.

Just as I started reading, a big ol' boy from New Jersey sat down beside me. How did I know Jeff was from Jersey? Because he told me so before he had even sat down. It didn't matter to him that I was working and had not even looked up at him. No. He felt the liberty to talk over the top of my concentration and to do so loudly and with a big smile on his face. He just couldn't help himself.

The reason I remember Jeff is because of the conversation that ensued. Early into the flight, he asked me about the book I was reading, and I explained that it addressed the question of whether human beings could know the truth about reality. Very soon I realized, in spite of myself, that this conversation was headed very quickly in a good direction and that God was breaking through my barriers so that I could be a conduit of the gospel for this man, Jeff.

It turns out that Jeff was in a perfect situation in life to receive the gospel. He and I talked about the gospel for the entire duration of the flight. Even during the meals. Eventually, I took out a sheet of paper and drew a diagram in which I attempted to teach him the meaning of the whole Bible, beginning at creation and ending with the new heavens and earth. But we focused on the Old Testament prophecies about Jesus, the life and ministry of Jesus, and the death and resurrection of Jesus.

In the middle of our conversation, Jeff found himself believing the gospel. God had prepared him for the gospel, had placed him beside me in an airplane, and had interrupted my preconceived plans, so that I could share with Jeff the good news.

By the time Jeff and I deplaned, I had his e-mail address. He and I interacted a couple more times. I helped him find a church in Jersey. He sent me a thank-you card and a gift. And so forth. But what he had given me unintentionally was a lifelong reminder to "always be prepared" for God-given opportunities.

> We are always on mission. We are always ambassadors for Christ, always called to represent Christ in our words and our deeds.

That is the point of this book. We are always on mission. We are always ambassadors for Christ, always called to represent Christ in our words and our deeds. We are "on-duty," not only when we are attending church or doing devotions, but also when we are at work, at home, or in the community. We are on-duty, not only if we are international missionaries or pastors but also if we are homemakers, scientists, or businessmen. There is no situation in which a Christian is "off-duty," and we should leverage the totality of our lives for the mission of God.

Where Are the Ends of the Earth?

After Jesus rose from the dead, he made appearances to his disciples. The author of Acts, a doctor named Luke, records Jesus' words to his disciples during one of those appearances. In that appearance, the disciples had asked Jesus when he would restore the kingdom. Jesus responded by saying

> "It is not for you to know times or periods that the Father has set by His own authority. But you will receive power when the Holy Spirit has come on you, and you will be My witnesses in Jerusalem, in all Judea and Samaria, and to the ends of the earth." (Acts 1:7–8)

In other words, Jesus told his disciples, "Stop trying to figure out time lines about when I'm going to return. That's not for you to worry about. The thing you should concentrate on is the one big task I've given you: being Spirit-empowered witnesses not only to the people of Israel, but also to all of the other nations. You should devote your lives—your words and your actions—to showing the world that I am King and Savior!"

Jesus' statement should not have been a surprise to the disciples. All along, God had told the Old Testament people of God (Israel) that they should be witnesses to him. "I will also make you a light for the nations, to be My salvation to the ends of the earth" (Isa. 49:6). All along, God had given instructions to Israel through the law, showing them how the totality of their lives—family, workplace, and community—should be a witness to him. And now, the Lord Jesus would tell the New Testament people of God (the church) to be a witness to the nations.

So Jesus' statement was not entirely new. But there was something new about it. Whereas in the Old Testament, God had emphasized that the nations would be *drawn to* Israel, now in the New Testament he is emphasizing that the New Testament people of God—the church—should *go to* the nations.

This missionary commission is so significant that Luke even organized the book of Acts around it. At the beginning of Acts, we see the triumph of the gospel in Jerusalem (Acts 2–7). Later in Acts, we see the gospel take hold in Judea and Samaria (Acts 8–12) and to the ends of the earth (Acts 13–28).

So if Jesus is commanding us to take the gospel to the ends of the earth, how should we define "the ends of the earth"? Who are "the nations"? The answer is that every nation that is not the Old Testament people of God is the "ends of the earth." God intends for his gospel to go to every nation, every group of people, across the face of the earth.

You see, those of us who live in America or Europe often misinterpret this passage. We view the West as "Jerusalem," and we treat Africa, Asia, and Latin America as if they were the "ends of the earth." But this is not the right way to look at it. In God's mind, Jerusalem represented Israel, who was the Old Testament people of God. Through Luke, he was saying, I will give the gospel to Israel first, but then after that I will send the gospel to the Gentile nations.

For those of us who live in North America or Europe, this is the point: together, our churches should make every effort to be witnesses to Christ, in our words and our actions, to every nation in the world, including our own nations. If we obey Christ, we will take the gospel to the ends of the earth, and if we take it to the ends of the earth we will be taking it not only to other nations but to our own.

How Can We Stay on Task?

If Jesus' imperative is so clear and obvious, what holds us back? Once again, we can learn from Doctor Luke. In the Gospel of Luke, he argues that we should be disciples of Christ. In Luke 14:25–33, he provides an insightful description of the nature of true discipleship. If we pay close attention to this description, we will discern some significant clues to why we tend to ignore Jesus' teaching to be gospel witnesses to all nations. Here is Luke's description of discipleship:

> [25]Now great crowds were traveling with Him. So He turned and said to them: [26]"If anyone comes to Me and does not hate his own father and mother, wife and children, brothers and sisters—yes, and even his own life—he cannot be My disciple. [27]Whoever does not bear his own cross and come after Me cannot be My disciple.
>
> [28]"For which of you, wanting to build a tower, doesn't first sit down and calculate the cost to see if he has enough to complete it? [29]Otherwise, after he has laid the foundation and cannot finish it, all the onlookers will begin to make fun of him, [30]saying, 'This man started to build and wasn't able to finish.'
>
> [31]"Or what king, going to war against another king, will not first sit down and decide if he is able with 10,000 to oppose the one who comes against him with 20,000? [32]If not, while the other is still far off, he sends a delegation and asks for terms of peace. [33]In the same

way, therefore, every one of you who does not say good-
bye to all his possessions cannot be My disciple."

Luke begins the passage by pointing out that enormous
crowds of people followed Jesus (v. 25), but that many of these
groupies weren't really disciples. They were just groupies. They
thought it was awesome to watch Jesus perform miracles (who
wouldn't want to see demons cast out of a man and into pigs,
and then to see the pigs doing backflips and cannonballs into
the sea?). They liked the power of his words, the feisty and
clever retorts he gave to hypocritical religious leaders, and the
compassion he showed to the sick and marginalized among
them.

But immediately after Luke points out that Jesus had
beaucoups of groupies, he throws a cold splash of reality on his
readers. He makes clear that being a groupie is not the same as
being a disciple or true follower of Christ. A disciple is a person
whose life takes on three characteristics.

1. **Must Love Jesus:** *The first characteristic of a true disciple
is that he loves Christ more than he loves any other person or thing.*
When Jesus says that his disciples must "hate" their family and
their friends, he is using the Hebrew sense of the word, which
means "to love less." Jesus doesn't intend for us to "hate" our
families in the English-language sense of that word. Instead, he
wants us to love, trust, and obey Jesus more than we love, trust,
or obey any other person or thing. Jesus is the supreme Lord of

the universe. What's more, he is the Lord who loved us enough to die on our behalf, to provide the way of salvation for us. In response to his lordship and Saviorship, we give to him our wholehearted love, trust, and obedience.

Jesus is not trying to tell us that if we love him better, we will love other people worse. In fact, the more we love him, the better we will love others. Our love for him will shape the way we love other people and things, and it will increase our love for those people and things. So Jesus is not instructing us to neglect or reject other people or other things that he has given us. He is instructing us to allow our love for him to infuse our lives so that it pours over into, and shapes our love for, the other good gifts that he has given us. As C. S. Lewis put it, "Aim at Heaven and you will get earth 'thrown in': aim at earth and you will get neither."[9]

Jesus is trying to tell us to stop loving people and things more than we love him. Any of the people or things that we are tempted to love more than we love Jesus are—ironically—gifts from Jesus. If we love our children more than we love Jesus, we should remember that Jesus is the one who gave us the children we have! If we love sex or money or success more than we love Jesus, we should remember that Jesus is the one who gave humanity the gifts of sex, money, and success. In other words, don't love the gift more than the Giver. Don't make a god out of something God created, out of something that is not God.

This characteristic of discipleship is very, very important. It is listed first because it is the most important and because the other characteristics flow from this one. If we are madly in love with sexual pleasure, or business success, or financial prosperity, we will inevitably not be focused on the Great Commission. Christians who are sidetracked by their flings with false gods will never stay on track to be the type of witnesses God wants us to be. The single most significant thing that holds us back from "going" is that we continually are tempted to love false gods more than we love God.

2. **Must Obey Jesus:** *The second characteristic of a true disciple is that he loves and obeys Jesus even in the midst of suffering and opposition.* In verse 27, Jesus says that we cannot be his disciples unless we are willing to carry a cross with us as we follow him. In Jesus' day, the cross was a brutal instrument of torture and execution. It was a symbol of Roman law, and of the consequences of breaking that law. It was not a quaint symbol or a cute decorative emblem. It was a symbol of death. So why would Jesus speak about discipleship in terms of a cross? He does so because his life and ministry was built on the fact that he—and not the Roman Caesar, or any other earthly ruler or god—is the supreme Lord of the universe. His claim to lordship was a direct affront to Caesar who viewed himself as supreme Lord. Jesus knew that this claim would lead to his death. And he knew that his disciples would also suffer and die because of it.

So the second characteristic expands upon the first characteristic. When we love, trust, and obey Jesus in an ultimate manner, that means that we will continue to love, trust, and obey him even when we face opposition or persecution because of it. As disciples, we realize that Jesus is the most valuable treasure that a person could possibly have. He is more valuable than anything else we could have or anything else that opposition or persecution could take away. And when the time comes that we are forced to choose between Jesus and popularity, between Jesus and wealth, between Jesus and freedom, or between Jesus and our family, we will choose Jesus.

We Americans could learn a lot from our brothers and sisters around the world. I am reminded of a story Nik Ripken tells in his book *The Insanity of God*. Ripken, a global missionary who is known for his research on Islam and on former Muslims who have embraced Jesus as Lord, asked one woman in China how believers were able to serve Christ in an environment with so little freedom. He recorded her response:

> The security police regularly harass a believer who owns the property where a house-church meets. The police say, "You have got to stop these meetings! If you do not stop these meetings, we will confiscate your house, and we will throw you out into the street."
>
> Then the property owner will probably respond, "Do you want my house? Do you want my farm? Well,

if you do, then you need to talk to Jesus because I gave this property to him."

The security police will not know what to make of that answer. So they will say, "We don't have any way to get to Jesus, but we can certainly get to you! When we take your property, you and your family will have nowhere to live!"

And the house-church believers will declare, "Then we will be free to trust God for shelter as well as for our daily bread."

"If you keep this up, we will beat you!" the persecutors will tell them.

"Then we will be free to trust Jesus for healing," the believers will respond.

"And then we will put you in prison!" the police will threaten.

By now, the believers' response is almost predictable: "Then we will be free to preach the good news of Jesus to the captives, to set them free. We will be free to plant churches in prison."

"If you try to do that, we will kill you!" the frustrated authorities will vow.

And, with utter consistency, the house-church believers will reply, "Then we will be free to go to heaven and be with Jesus forever."[10]

3. **Must Never Quit:** *The third characteristic of a disciple is that he or she is not a quitter.* In verses 28–32, Jesus tells two stories that illustrate the same point: disciples of Christ must "count the cost" when they decide to get baptized and declare to the world that they are Christians. They must be prepared to embrace Christ for the duration. When we declare to the world that we are disciples of Christ, we are declaring that Jesus Christ is the one true God, that he is worthy of our love and worship, and that we will never tarnish his name by quitting the path of discipleship.

Disciples will often face the temptation to forsake Christ for some other "god." They will be faced at every turn with the temptation to trust, love, and obey some other "lord." They will be tempted to cling to the pleasures of illicit sex, the comfort of financial wealth, the allure of success, or the supposed security of positions of power. But if we succumb to these temptations, we are implicitly declaring that "Christ is not really enough. In order to be truly happy or truly secure, I must have _____, which functions as my true savior." To take our feet off the path of discipleship is to imply that Christ is not Lord.

Luke concludes the passage by saying that a disciple is a person who believes Jesus is Lord, and who, for that reason, forsakes everything else in order to love, trust, and obey Jesus. Conversely, a person who believes Jesus is Lord is one who refuses to make a "god" out of anything or anybody else in life.

What Is Holding Us Back?

Pause for a moment and think about the idols in your life that vie with the Lord for your heart's affections. Is *sexual pleasure* your functional savior? When you take the good gift of sex and make it into a god, it will derail and destroy your life. Sex is a good gift from God when it is practiced lovingly in a committed marriage, but it is a tool of Satan when it is practiced in any other manner. In fact, it is one of Satan's handiest tools when distracting Christians from the mission of God. If the Evil One can distract us with pornography, casual sexual encounters, and adulterous relationships, he can easily take our eyes off the mission.

Have *money and possessions* become your functional savior? Some people—we'll call them the "spenders"—idolize money in a more obvious manner. They love money so much because they think it will buy things that will make them truly happy. For these people, the things money can buy, such as fashionable clothes, nice cars, and fancy houses, are their functional saviors. But spenders aren't the only people who idolize money; the "savers" do also. Savers love money so much because they think that if they save their money, if they invest for the future, their lives will be secure and they will have nothing to worry about. The thing that is similar about spenders and savers is that both look to money to give them something only Christ can give— true and lasting happiness or true and lasting security. If we are busy obsessing on money, we will likely never open ourselves to the possibility of becoming international missionaries or the opportunity to leverage our workplace talents for God and his mission.

Is *success* the driving factor in your life? This is a destructive form of idolatry that often passes as a harmless desire to provide for family or excel in the workplace. In this scenario, a person judges his self-worth by whether or not he succeeds in classes, work, or some other area of his life. A college student might neglect her family, friends, and church, shoving all of these to the side so that she can make "A"s in every course. A businessman might ignore his wife and children over the course of his career so that he can climb to the top of his field. But this sort of success comes at the expense of God's best for us: he wishes for us to seek him and his Kingdom first, and if we do that, he will add all of these things in their own time.

This list could easily be multiplied: family, comfort, leisure, sports, romance, power, friendship, a political affiliation, prestige, and the approval of other people. If it's a good thing, it's a candidate for idolatry. *Any* gift of God, when elevated to the level of godship, becomes idolatrous, destructive, even demonic. In fact, the better the raw material, the stronger the idol.

Remember: when we allow any created thing or person to gain the status of an "idol" in our lives, what we are saying to the world is that this thing or person is more valuable than

God himself. We are saying that God cannot really save us, and that we need this thing or person to save us and bring us the happiness, the security, the peace we really crave. And, devastatingly, these idols each provide us with distinctive missions. Rather than being witnesses for God, we become witnesses to sex or money or power. Or whatever it is we idolize.

For this reason, when we experience the seductive allure of idols, therefore, we realize what is at stake. We should determine not to allow anything or anyone to have the status of "God" in our lives—except, of course, for God himself. We should determine to love, trust, and obey him more than we love, trust, or obey these other things. When we love God in this way, and when we allow him to shape the way we love other people and things, then we are able to truly promote Christ with our lives while we are proclaiming him with our lips. Only then can our words and our lives form a seamless testimony to the greatness of God in Christ. Only then can we truly and fully join God on his mission.

Concluding Challenge

Our friend David Platt is a prime example of a man willing to go anywhere. Before he surrendered—and it was surrender— to serve as president of the IMB, he was wrestling with God, willing to leave an effective ministry in the United States to live and work among people far away from home. David knows what we know—going is not a sacrifice when the gospel becomes your greatest treasure.

Because the gospel is David's greatest pleasure, leading a missions agency—even the largest in the world—pales in comparison to serving God anywhere he leads. In order to lead, even a prestigious post like the IMB presidency, God would have to tell David to "go." Because the gospel is David's greatest treasure—not comfort, money, ministry success, family, or anything else—David told God, "Yes" to the call to go anywhere.

Will you go anywhere?

God may be calling you to go across the ocean or across the street. He may be calling you to the Congo or a cubicle. Will you go anywhere he leads?

On the back of this little book you will find something unusual. Unlike some authors, we want you to write all over the (back) cover of our book. The back cover says, "I Am Going to" and leaves room for you to fill in the blank. If you have read this book—I think it's safe to assume you have at this point—it is likely that you have gained some sense of clarity of where God is leading. For some, you may have confirmed what you already knew before: God is leading you where you already are. For others, you have finally risked believing that God is leading you to go somewhere new. Either way, you are going. We want to know where!

Fill in the blank. Where are you going?

Tweet us a picture of the back of your book. Email us. Take a picture and mail it to us. We want to know.

_____

_____

Sign the pledge:

I, _____, will go anywhere.

Notes

1. Mark Dever, *The Gospel Made Visible* (Nashville, TN: B&H Publishing Group, 2012), 10.

2. John Calvin, *Calvin: Institutes of the Christian Religion*, Volume 2, ed. John T. McNeill (Louisville, KY: Westminster John Knox Press, 2006), 1031.

3. The descriptions of local churches in the New Testament assume that these local, visible congregations are composed of believers only. The church of God in Corinth is called "those who are sanctified in Christ Jesus" (1 Cor. 1:2). The letter to the Ephesians is addressed to "the faithful saints in Christ Jesus at Ephesus" (Eph. 1:1). The letter to the church in Philippi is sent "to all the saints in Christ Jesus" (Phil. 1:1). Paul wrote "to the saints in Christ at Colosse, who are faithful brothers" (Col. 1:2). The church of the Thessalonians is described in both letters as a church "in God the Father and the Lord Jesus Christ" (1 Thess. 1:1; 2 Thess. 1:2).

4. Dietrich Bonhoeffer, *The Cost of Discipleship* (New York, NY: Simon and Schuster, 2010), 89–90, italics mine.

5. Kuyper spoke these words during an inaugural address at the Free University of Amsterdam, which he founded. His remarks can be found in Kuyper, "Sphere Sovereignty," in *Abraham Kuyper: A Centennial Reader*, ed. James D. Bratt (Grand Rapids, MI: Eerdmans, 1998), 488.

6. From an excerpt of Abraham Kuyper, *Pro Rege,* translated by Jan Boer, *You Can Do Greater Things than Christ* (Nigeria: Jos, 1991).

7. Martin Luther, exposition of 1 Peter 2:18–20, as excerpted in *What Luther Says*, 15001501.

8. Richard Sibbes, *King David's Epitaph,* in *The Complete Works of Richard Sibbes* (Edinburgh: James Nichol, 1863), 6:507.

9. C. S. Lewis, *Mere Christianity* (San Francisco, CA: Harper Collins, 2009), 134.

10. Nik Ripken, *The Insanity of God: A True Story of Faith Resurrected* (Nashville, TN: B&H Publishing Group, 2013), 262–63.

LIMITLESS

OPPORTUNITIES

The world is full of limitless opportunities.

How is God calling you and your church
to fulfill Christ's commission?

INTERNATIONAL MISSION BOARD

IMB partners with churches to empower limitless missionary
teams who are making disciples and multiplying churches
among unreached peoples and places for the glory of God.

God has burdened your heart
for those who have yet to hear
the loving message of the gospel.

You want to make a difference.

LOTTIE MOON CHRISTMAS OFFERING®

Give to the Lottie Moon Christmas Offering to send
and support missionaries who are going to difficult
places, overcoming obstacles to proclaim Jesus to
the unreached. 100% of your giving goes directly to
support this work around the world.

imb.org/give

imb
INTERNATIONAL
MISSION BOARD